выписал[и] ... ...трес
пункт. ... направлении, ... в ...
таках [же] как ... выздоравливающих ... мы повс[е]
приближающийся к нам кавалерии. И когда уже мо[г]
лица я узнал в начальнике своего командира эскадр[она]
Твар. Кирасе[с]ского полка полк. Михайлова, к[оторому]
я обратился с просьбой указать нам [как] нам лучш[е]
командир приказал нам итти за эскадроном ..
том случае нам будет возможность погрузиться н[а]
вальщик завтра в Крым. Проведя ночь в одном
на[ходящ]их находящихся на пристани, на другой день
на пароход "Тигр" и отплыли по направлению [в]
Крым. [...] Во время плавания со мной случ[ился]
тифа и я не помню как и что со мной происх[одило]
прикасали подготовившись к высадке я уже был в
и собирая свои скудные пожитки и одевая наше с[о]
другого, при всем своем старании и содействии
так и не удалось. Один из близ[стоящ]их солдат ..
какие то полурезиновые, полу полотняные баш[маки]
с большой благодарностью принял, что бы не-
Вид[а] Высадка произошла в порту гор. Фео[досия]
был выдан белый, пшеничный Крымский хлеб и ...
и "Камса" мелкая соленая рыбешка т.к. все мы были
Камса оказалось нам очень вкусной. На Феодосий[ской]

Memoirs of a White Russian

Efimij, age 39

Efimij Mokrij

Memoirs of a White Russian

2013

First edition 2013.
Published in the USA.

Authored by Efimij Mokrij (original Russian). Translated by Rosh Ireland. Edited and proofed by Tanya Spisbah, Natasha Mokrij, Noel Riley, Peter Pullicino (chief editor). Interior design by Peter Pullicino. Cover art by Polina Vladimirovna Ipatova, Zaporozhye, Ukraine. Cover design by Peter Pullicino. Translation of 1932 letter from the Serbian by Katarina Stevanovic (Serbia).

Footnotes are editorial.

Publication data

Mokrij, Efimij V (1903 - 1989)
        Memoirs of a White Russian
1.   Russian Civil War – Southern Russia 2. White Russian movement - White Russian émigré 3. Russian Liberation movement 4 Russian Corps – Serbia. 5 Russian House – Australia.

ISBN-13: 978-1482570595
ISBN-10: 1482570599

Contents

Preface

Efimij Mokrij was my paternal grandfather. I remember him as a kind and generous man who doted on his two grandchildren, my brother Maxim and I. I spent a lot of time with him and my grandmother, Slava, during my childhood in Melbourne and later when we all moved to Canberra. We visited their home often, and they would always spoil and shower us with gifts and money. They themselves lived very modestly and frugally. I remember how my grandfather would travel long distances, usually by foot as they never owned a car, whenever there was a bargain to be had. I would also see him at church, where he and my grandmother went every Sunday without fail.

He never spoke about his time as a White Russian soldier - at least not to me.

My grandfather considered that a university education was crucial. He would talk to me at length about the importance of continuing my education and the many benefits that it would confer on my life. . His war service disrupted his own studies and I think that this was a source of some sadness to him. He was very pleased that his son, Alexander, my father, was able to complete a Masters degree. He hoped that I would do the same. Both he and Slava passed away in 1989 during my first year of university. He was so pleased that I had gone, though unfortunately he didn't get to see me receive my Masters degree some years later.

My grandfather wrote his memoirs in 1976 and although I was aware of their existence when I was growing up, I hadn't read them as they were written in Russian. Before my father passed away in late 2009 he wrote his own memoirs and reminded me of my grandfather's. After my father's passing, I decided to find a translator to translate my grandfather's memoirs into English. A few years later, a dear friend of mine, Peter Pullicino, who had played a part in organising the translator, offered his help in putting the memoirs into the form of a book for publishing. He took this task on with great fervour and it is largely thanks to him that it's in this form today.

A special thank you to Tanya Spisbah, for her dedication in editing the proof. I would like to thank my husband, Noel Riley, for all his valuable input, which included editing as well as endless advice. Thanks also to Rosh Ireland for translating Efimij's memoirs into English.

I look forward to the time when my own children, Blake and Charlotte, are able to read these memoirs and learn about their great grandfather and his life journey.

Natasha Mokrij
Canberra, 2013

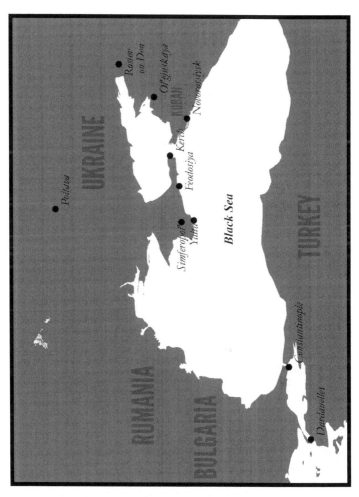

Map1. From Ukraine to Turkey.

1

From Poltava to Kraljevo

Part 1

'Ya Mokry'

In the years of our youth, seldom would one of us attach any importance to events taking place around us, though they affect not only people unconnected with us, but also ourselves. When, however, old age comes close and the end of our life on this earth approaches, the question arises unasked: for what did I live in this world; what meaning was there in my life and have I left any trace which would be of benefit to those close to me ('according to the teaching of the Bible')?

These questions bring me willy-nilly to the thought of recalling the distant past of this family of ours, the 'Mokry', gleaned by me from the words of my relatives and friends and of friends of our family.

According to the old people, who supposedly knew the roots of our family, our ancestors came from the Zaporozhians and that section of the free peoples which would not submit to the Poles, the Tartars or the Turks. I will not attempt to describe the way of life of these people, since it is well known to me and to many of us from history and is particularly well described by our beloved writer Nikolai Vasilievich Gogol.

According to my older relatives, and particularly their friends, my ancestors, the Zaporozhians, were avid roisterers in the Cossack manner. One merrymaker, failing to keep his feet, tumbled into the Dnieper, and after this unfortunate dip was drying himself in the sun. At that very time a census of the Cossack host was being made by government order and the commission, coming across this young fellow, tried to establish his surname to enter it in the list. Asked for his surname, the Cossack, half asleep, kept repeating, '*ya mokry*' - 'I'm wet'. Having obtained no more satisfactory answer, the commission decreed that 'Cossack Mokry' be entered. I will not try either to confirm or contest the truth of this evidence; I leave it to the conscience of my elders.

I have documentary confirmation that, in my time, our family was officially regarded as 'Cossack'. Thus the pre-revolutionary birth certificate reads: first name–Yevfimy; father–Cossack Vasily Davydovich Mokry; mother–Cossack Akelina Stepanovna Chepizhskaya etc. That birth certificate is in my possession.

I now move to a description of my late grandfather, my father and mother and other family members.

My late grandfather, David Fedorovich, was born in the reign of Emperor Nicholas I in 1854, if I am correct, during the Crimean War. He was called up into the army in 1875. Having been a regular in the Volynsky regiment of the Life Guards in Warsaw and having served two years, he was posted with his regiment to the Balkan front, where he took part in the battles for Plevna and the Shipka pass (in Bulgaria), for which he received decorations.

After the war, after two years at the front, he was posted back to Warsaw, where he served a further two years. At that time service with the regular army was six years. My late grandfather was the youngest of six brothers and, returning from military service and receiving his portion of the inheritance, he soon married and began a family. He did not stay long in his home district, where there was no opportunity to strike out and establish oneself. He and a friend soon found a suitable large block of land 20 versts away.[1] Selling their own land, they bought the block, settled there, worked together with enthusiasm, quickly became rich and gradually bought up fresh blocks from neighbouring landowners, taking advantage of the favourable terms of the state bank under the Stolypin plan. As the property developed, so the family grew. The first son, my father, had already, as a youngster, started school. Then came three sisters and finally a younger brother, Fedor. It was then, however, that a great misfortune overtook my grandfather. My grandmother died, leaving grandfather with 5 children, the eldest 10 years old and the youngest 3 months!

---

[1] 1 verst is slightly more than 1 km.

My grandfather did not lose heart. He firmly refused to marry again, as importunate neighbours urged, so as to have someone to leave the children with. 'I don't want a stepmother for my children. I'll cope as well as I can myself.'

A heavy burden fell on his shoulders. According to the neighbours' accounts, he would get up very early, especially in summer when work in the fields had to be done, prepared food for children and himself, cleaned the house, fed the stock and went out into the fields, and went to bed late, when all the work in and around the house was finished and the children were put to bed. This life, full of labour and deprivations, went on for seven years. When my father was seventeen, grandfather, having got permission from the Bishop in charge of the dioceses, married his son to my late mother, Akelina, with the laudable objective of bringing a housewife into the house. A year later a daughter was born, eighteen months after that a son (myself), and later three more daughters. When I was fifteen and a half, my mother died after a long and painful disease of the lungs.

Our family was very religious. As a rule, each member of the family and we children gathered to pray morning and evening. The children could not yet read the prayers for themselves and repeated the words of the prayers after one of the older people, mainly mother. Our family regularly went to church, despite the distance – from three to seven versts. The nearest, in a colony of retired railwaymen, was three versts away, and the six churches in the district town of Kobelyaki were seven versts away. Most frequently they went on horseback, when they would take us

18

children as well, but the grown-ups sometimes went on foot; grandfather did so particularly often.

We children were very fond of grandfather, since he was always giving us presents, usually sweets, and spoiled us far more than father, who was stricter with us, especially with me, since I was very mischievous. I cannot say why it was that grandfather was very religious; possibly it was the influence of his parents, whom I did not know, since, at the time I remember, they were no longer living.

On the other hand, I remember my maternal grandfather and his family well. My maternal grandmother was no longer alive. My mother had four brothers and four sisters. The whole family was also highly religious. The elder brother was sexton-precentor in a suburb of Poltava, Rybtsy; his sons were at the seminary in Poltava and the daughters at the diocesan school in the same town. One brother was a rural medic; one had dedicated himself to the Lord in the local church and was not married; only one of them was fully engaged in work on the property, which he managed successfully, replacing his old father. Most probably I also have inherited a touch of religiosity from my parents and relatives. My late mother often read the Bible to us children and much has remained until now in my memory.

At an early age (about four to five years) my mother began to teach me and my eldest sister to read, so that, when we went to school, we could already read, which made our schooling much easier. When I finished primary school, a family council resolved to give me the opportunity to continue study. After some preparation, I entered the local Classical Gymnasium, which I went through with great success. At that time the war had already begun, and as a result the course of events changed greatly. In 1914, my uncle was called up. On 6 January 1915, my father was mobilised (by that time all three of my father's sisters were married) and on our property, large for the times, there remained only my sixty-year-old grandfather and his twelve-year-old grandson (myself), my mother and my four sisters, the eldest of whom was thirteen. This was not an impressive work force; all had to use their full strength and ability in order not to let the property run down. I had to spend my school holidays on heavy work in the fields and help my grandfather to run the property.

In June 1915 we were informed that my uncle had been killed in an attack on the Galician front. At that time, my father was on the German front in Poland. After a long interval, a letter came from my father in Moscow. He was in hospital, wounded in the right hand. A bullet had gone right through his palm, shattering as it exited the bone of the thumb and damaging the tendons of the other fingers. My father was soon invalided home. Before the war began, my father had joined up with two of his friends and they were engaged in various kinds of small-scale trade. He kept this up after he came back from the war. This somewhat compensated for his inability to play his full part on the property, because of his crippled right hand. Family life went on almost normally.

Returning to my personal life; I successfully completed the course at the Gymnasium (I was one of the best pupils), and during the holidays was fully occupied with work on the property. When I finished third class with a First Class Award (and a gold medal), with the permission of the Director of the

Gymnasium I completed the fourth class course in the three-and-a-half months of the summer holidays and, passing the examination, went into fifth class.

The Civil War

My education continued normally and successfully until the revolution, or rather until the arrival of the Bolsheviks, when various unpleasantnesses began. My father was soon arrested for not paying the contribution levied on him. As a boy, I had to do the rounds of various offices to try to get him freed. My father was finally freed, paying a reduced contribution. This was in early 1918. We were soon liberated from the Communists by Hetman Skoropadsky's troops in alliance with the Germans. The summer passed peacefully, but in the autumn the Germans left, following events in Germany. They were replaced for a few weeks by the Petlyurovtsy[2], and they in their turn by the Reds. The contribution business was repeated for my father; this time it was larger.

In the spring of 1919, the White Army arrived. Our district was occupied by the 2nd Terskaya Division and everything seemed to settle down, but not for long. When the White Army moved further north, pursuing the Reds, the Makhnovtsy[3] began raiding in their rear. Their raids were violent; hence when they appeared many inhabitants (including the pupils of the senior class in the Gymnasium and the Commercial School) would retreat from the town as

---

[2] Ukrainian nationalists.

[3] Peasant anarchists allied with Nestor Ivanovych Makhno. The Makhnovtsy harassed the Whites relentlessly.

they approached, together with the (small) garrison). They did not always manage to do this, since the Makhnovtsy would appear unexpectedly.

Following one of these retreats, we did not return, since the White Army made a hurried withdrawal from the areas it had occupied. In the autumn of 1919 many of us, myself included, volunteered for the White Army, hoping that we would soon be able to return home[4]. The optimists even assumed that this would happen within a few days, but none of us knew the situation that had developed. Perhaps the officers knew, but no one said anything about it to us.

All we senior pupils etc. were dressed as if we were setting off for school or for a walk, without money, without any change of clothing, which soon had its effect on the march. In Poltava I met some friends from the Gymnasium who had earlier joined the 1st Guards Composite Cuirassier Regiment, and I also joined that regiment. They also were hoping to be back soon.

Soon we received our arms: British rifles and bamboo lances. We were mounted on horses and moved off in column to the south. I was very fond of horses and since childhood had loved riding, but ten to fifteen hours at a time in the saddle was new to me! It began to rain; frosts followed; the march became more and more arduous. When we stopped, shelter and feed had to found for the horse and it had to be rubbed down. Then one had to think of oneself, of

---

[4] The peak of the White advance came in October 1919, when they were 380km from Moscow, but it was rapidly downhill from November 1919 onwards.

food and of somewhere to sleep. Thus we crossed the Ukrainian lands and entered the Don region[5].

Periodically those more familiar with military training were taken from our reserve squadron to be sent as reinforcements to the front. We raw recruits were not yet so honoured. Occasionally we were given the opportunity to relax a little, clean ourselves up and wash our underclothes (if anyone had a spare set). There were always kind women who were willing to help us out.

After a day, we moved on. In Rostov-on-Don we stopped for several days; horse numbers and weaponry were made up and we received some uniform items such as underwear. It was December, with Christmas only a few days away. We moved on. On Christmas Eve we arrived at the stanitsa of Olginskaya, which was crammed with troops. It was vain to think of any comforts, or indeed of food. With great difficulty we somewhere got hold of some flour and made *galushki* [dumplings] for supper, instead of the traditional splendid Christmas Eve dinner. We had to sleep sitting on the floor, packed shoulder to shoulder. The horses also were poorly fed. In the morning we moved on in the direction of the Kuban. Not far from the Kuban region we passed a distillery and the bibulous amongst us paid it a visit, some remaining there for a considerable time. Our squadron missed one of the regular troop NCOs, who appeared the next day drunk and under escort. When he sobered up, the CO paraded the squadron, placed the miscreant facing it, read the charge and, pointing out that this was not his first offence, despite

---

[5] This would have been a journey of 500km to 700km depending where Efimij was when the White front collapsed.

frequent warnings, ordered him to be stripped of his badges of rank and – told him to clear off!

I have to say that, to my great regret and to our shame and disgrace, drunkenness, theft and various misdemeanours greatly undermined the authority of the White Army, and the population would frequently complain, saying: 'what difference is there between you and the Bolsheviks? Though it is true that in most cases they robbed the rich and you the poor – often taking their last possessions…'

And, regretfully one must admit that there is a great deal of truth in that. There were orders not to steal, but how can one keep an eye on everyone?

Battles in the Kuban region

So we crossed into the rich region of the Kuban. Passing through the stanitsas, we reached Pereyaslavskaya and stayed there for a longer period. Preparations were being made to push back the advancing Red Army and our squadron was to provide considerable reinforcements, amongst whom was myself. We were kitted out, provided with arms and better horses and awaited the order to move.

For some reason the order was delayed and in the meantime several men, including myself, were taken to hospital with typhus. I had the first attack of recurring typhus. Hence, when the reinforcements moved off, I was in bed with a temperature of about 40. Within a few days the fever passed, but the second soon followed and then the third and fourth, during which (according to the Cossack housewife) I was unconscious. The misfortune did not end there, since dysentery followed and, when one takes into account very poor care on the part of the housewife, who was practically all the time busy outside and inside the house, my position was desperate. There were no medicines apart from aspirin and quinine (from which I became almost deaf) and the nurse who did the rounds of patients would spread her arms in despair, saying, 'I have absolutely nothing to help you with'.

I now return to the reinforcements, which went off to the front without me and the others. It was January[6]. It had snowed heavily and there was a thick frost. The cavalry regiments were concentrating. According to those who were there, 42,000 men had concentrated on our side and 48,000 on the Reds' (it is possible that I have reversed those figures, but the numbers I remember well.) Battle was joined, during which, those who were there say, the flank where the Kuban units were stationed retreated. It was said that the Kuban units refused to fight, because, just before, the Kuban Military Council had been either arrested or dismissed. The Red cavalry began to encircle the units which had held their ground; there was confusion; units ran in order to avoid encirclement. They were partially successful, but the battle was lost. Some of our reinforcements returned frostbitten to the squadron and gave us eyewitness accounts of what had happened[7].

After the defeat at the stanitsa of Yagorlytskaya (if my memory does not deceive me, that was the name of the stanitsa), our units began to retreat into

---

[6] January 1920 - the Whites were holding out in the Don region.

[7] The confused battles for Rostov and Yagorlytskaya (aka Egorlykskaia) during early 1920 were fought in -26°C/-15°F degree temperatures. Men and horses froze to death (Mawdsley: 307).

the Kuban region. Our sick and wounded began to be sent off in batches to Novorossiisk. I found myself in a party of thirty-six, most of whom could not walk. I was amongst those who could, since, after the fifth fever, the succeeding ones were already much milder. We were given one fit escort, who was given money and some food supplies, and loaded into a goods wagon (admittedly it had a stove) and sent off towards Novorossiisk.

Our journey to Novorossiisk turned out to be very long and arduous. Our escort soon disappeared, together with the money given us for food supplies. We moved extremely slowly. At every station our wagon was shunted into sidings. We had to work hard to persuade the railway officials to send us on. We had no idea whether this was sabotage or for some other reason. Our companions began to die. The railway officials refused to take out their bodies, advising us to toss them out of the train when it was moving. After a long ordeal, and with great difficulty, we reached Novorossiisk, sick, dirty, exhausted and starving. There we turned to the Red Cross, from which we received what help was possible in those conditions. The corpses were removed; we were all fed; we got some medical assistance. The serious cases were taken to hospitals, while those who were regarded as convalescent were advised to spend the night in the station buildings and get food from the Red Cross kitchen. Within a few days my legs swelled up and I could hardly move. I went to a Red Cross doctor, who sent me to a military hospital located in hangars with concrete floors, on which the sick and wounded lay packed together on straw mattresses.

Conditions in this hospital were desperate, as in all half-broken, retreating armies.

Within a few days or perhaps weeks, I don't remember, I began to recover and, on the doctor's advice, I began to walk outside with difficulty on my painful legs, swollen as they were like sacks of grain. The doctor turned out to be right. My legs gradually gained strength. The swelling went down. Soon, with other convalescents, I was discharged from the hospital and sent to a distribution centre. While we were going to where we had been directed, I, with a number of other convalescents like myself, met a party of cavalry coming towards us. When it became possible to make out the faces, I recognised the commanding officer as my own squadron commander, Colonel Mikhaylov of the Life Guards Cuirassier Regiment.

I asked him how we should proceed. The colonel ordered us to follow the squadron, since only thus would we be able to board a steamer departing the next day for the Crimea. Spending the night in one of the empty wagons standing on the jetty, the next day we boarded the steamer *Tiger* and sailed for the Crimean peninsula[8]. I had another attack of typhus during the voyage and could neither remember what happened to me or how it happened, but, however, when we were ordered to prepare to disembark, I was already fully conscious. As I was collecting my few possessions and dressing, I could find only one of my boots; for all my efforts and help

[8] This was probably in late March 1920. The Reds captured 22,000 troops left in Novorossiisk, but others fled down the coast. In late April 60,000 Whites surrendered at Sochi (Mawdsley: 308).

from my neighbours, I could not find the other. One of my neighbours offered me some half-rubber, half-cotton slippers, which I took most gratefully, so as not to have to go barefoot. We disembarked in the port of Feodosiya, where we were given luxuries: white Crimean bread and what in the Crimea is called *kamsa*, a small salted fish. As we were famished, the kamsa was delicious.

From Feodosiya we were sent on carts to some large village, the name of which I do not remember, where the process began of ridding us of all kinds of parasites. My Gymnasium overcoat was sheepskin, which had saved me from the cold during the campaign and later in the cold wagon, but, at the same time, had served as a nest for insects. There was no option but to burn it and everything in it. All my other clothing suffered the same fate. I was issued underclothes, a short coat which did not reach my knees, and a British army cap for my head. That was my entire uniform.

Because of a new attack of typhus, I was soon sent with others who were sick to a hospital situated in the large house of some landowner in the German colony with the Tartar name *Cherkes-Tabay*. The patients lay on the floor on straw mattresses. They were looked after by medical orderlies and treated by two nurses. Occasionally a doctor would come from somewhere. Some of the patients were exposed to draughts and easily caught colds - four of us went down with inflammation of the lungs. Two were treated by one of the sisters with cupping-jars. I and one other were treated by the other sister with compresses. As the orderlies explained, those who had been treated with the cupping-jars had evidently been exposed to draughts and soon died. We who had been treated with compresses, survived.

My illness, now in its sixth month, was coming to an end, but I was so weak that I could not stand up. When they got me up to move just a little, once I had made a couple of steps I would fall down and be unable to get myself up. But youth won out. I was seventeen and, either at the end of June or the beginning of July, I was discharged from hospital and sent to my regiment. A few weeks later I was assigned to a reserve squadron to be trained as reinforcements, but, a few days later, the first order was cancelled and we were all hastily transferred to Simferopol, where three training detachments were being formed, mainly of volunteers: the first of the line (to which I was assigned), the second a machine-gun detachment, and the third signals.

There were less than three weeks to go before training was to begin on 1 September, and I was assigned to a party of five to transport uniforms and arms to Kerch for a landing on the Taman peninsula in the Kuban. When we reached Kerch, we discovered that the landing force had been unsuccessful and had not found reliable support on the spot, and was returning to Kerch; we were ordered to return to Simferopol. Once we had returned to the training detachment, serious drills began to train future cadres for the army's cavalry units. However, although our forces were advancing successfully and there was hope that they would soon enter Kiev, something happened which hitherto had been regarded as inconceivable: the Polish government, despite their defeat of the Red Army, made peace with the Bolsheviks, and the whole mass of the Red Army, and above all Budenny's cavalry[9], was thrown south against the Whites, and our side began to retreat. The Army High Command resolved on evacuation of as many units as possible, since the fleet was in our hands and would be able to provide transport.

The order, strictly 'secret', was received at night. That night I was doing duty for the detachment and was one of the first to learn of it from the regimental duty officer. In the early morning the commander of the detachment, Captain Rozanov, came to the barracks, paraded the detachment and, explaining the situation, said: 'All of you who wish to be evacuated are to be ready, since, within hours, we shall move out of the town towards one of the ports for embarkation on steamers; those of you who are thinking of remaining here in the Crimea, those who consider that they will be able to manage to get home as local people, may leave when they have handed in their weapons. It is particularly important that none of those who wish to stay should take horses, since we are short of them and they must be distributed to those who have to make their way to a port for embarkation on the steamers'.

Swift exit from Yalta

The barracks hummed like a beehive when danger threatened. Within a few hours the barracks emptied and all the military units left the town, heading for Yalta. Two detachments were formed

---

[9] Semyon Mikhailovich Budyonny, Red commander of the 1st Cavalry Army.

from cavalry units with horses: one for the advance guard and the second for the rear-guard. The column moved off. As we approached Yalta, I, with others picked by the commander, was assigned as quartermaster and we rode ahead towards Yalta. As we neared Yalta, all the roads were full of retreating troops. It was vain to think of carrying out our orders to find quarters for our column. We quartermasters decided to halt and wait for the column. Here there occurred something unexpected which could have changed my destiny i.e. have prevented me from embarking on the steamer. I caught the eye of some colonel, who asked which was my unit and what was I doing here. When he learnt my unit and that I was a quartermaster, he said that my mission was over, since there was no point even of thinking of quarters, but that I would instead join this squadron on foot and go to the outpost. Then there appeared some captain to whom the colonel indicated me as messenger between the outpost and the port. So I went willy-nilly with this squadron to the outpost at Livadiya.

The squadron took up quarters in once comfortable, now deserted, buildings to guard the roads leading to the waterfront. Since I had nothing to do, I looked for whatever feed I could find for the horse. My duty was basically to maintain communication between the outpost and the transport commander, General Kreyter (who is still living in the USA).

Every morning and evening I rode to the General at the port and gave an oral report of everything I was ordered to by the outpost commander, and then in reverse reported the General's orders to the outpost commander. We were there for three days, and when, in the evening, I made my last report to the General, he sent this order to the outpost commander:

'Tomorrow at 1200, when you hear a second blast on the steamer's whistle, withdraw the outpost and move to the port for embarkation'. When he heard this order, the outpost commander remarked in disgust,

'Blow you, General, sir. You want to throw us to the Reds to save yourself. That won't happen. Tomorrow morning after breakfast we shall withdraw the outpost and head for the jetty!'

Indeed, in the morning, after breakfasting on what little we had, we headed for the Yalta waterfront. As we entered the town, we found total confusion: some were wandering about the town; some were taking what they could from open shops and pubs. Many were drunk, since an open wine warehouse had been ransacked for spirits. Some were handing out bottles to our column as it marched past; I had two bottles handed to me. When we had forced our way through the mob to the steamer, we found that the gangway had already been raised.

The outpost commander began to demand that the gangway be lowered to embark his squadron, but the reply was that the steamer was already overloaded and that General Kreyter, the convoy commander, had ordered that no more should be taken on board. When the squadron commander threatened that he would open fire with all weapons on the steamer (the squadron had machine guns), a General appeared, who, in view of the situation, ordered a rope ladder to be lowered, by which one by one we climbed onto the steamer. With pain in my heart I parted with my horse, who had served me faithfully from Simferopol to Yalta, and gave it to the first of those close by who asked for it – perhaps it served him too, possibly even better than it did me.

I have just remembered an interesting coincidence, perhaps more than that. When the training detachment was formed, as right marker I was given the best horse, a tall chestnut called Astra. She reminded me of my father's horses. I was very fond of her, since she was handsome and obedient. I often took her for rides. When we left Simferopol in column for Yalta, my troop commander, Captain Radionov, wanted my Astra for himself and gave me instead a small black horse, Angel. This Angel carried me safely to Yalta and right up to the steamer. Thus he helped me to escape the fate suffered by many of my comrades who remained in the Crimea – in their homeland.

Angel was the only living creature to whom I said farewell as I left the last inch of Russian soil.

To Gallipoli

2 November, 1920, 12 noon.

The fateful days had come for all those on the steamer. The steamer gave a deep blast on its whistle and a second one two minutes later, the screw turned and we slowly sailed off into the unknown. It was only now that we came to realise what had been in store for us if our outpost commander had obeyed the General's order. We would indeed have been thrown to the Reds to save him. Our gratitude goes to that officer with the foresight to save us from massacre by the Reds.

Meeting here in Australia people who witnessed our evacuation in 1920, I learnt that, after we had left the Crimea, there followed a savage and persistent hunt for all those who, in one degree or another, cooperated with or were members of the White Army, and mountains of corpses were revenge for fighting against Bolshevism. Thus ended three years of fighting in the south of Russia.

When one begins in cold blood to discuss some event, one invariably finds a justification even for a bad action, taking account of the situation, a man's mental state, his feelings, the psychological moment, the state of the nervous system etc.

In our 'Russian tragedy', from my point of view, blame falls not on one man, one class or social group, one nationality, but on almost all of us, children excluded, with very few exceptions. 'Divine punishment' fell on almost all of us, as once it fell on the Jewish people! And what more could we have expected? Some remained to pay for their actions in their homeland, others in exile. The first fell into the iron grip of their own people, often their own brothers or sisters. The others, escaping, forgot or tried to forget their past sins and misdemeanours and by whatever means to regain what they had lost, totally forgetting their duty to their brothers and their homeland! And, most important, the transitory nature of all that is earthly. For some reason, we strive to catch up and overtake each other in material things, earthly rewards etc.

If we begin to work on some good and useful cause, there is inevitably an immediate reaction, either from envy or from someone's thought that they will be worse off. It is so almost everywhere: whatever you do you cannot win! It often happens that people who have done a great deal for society come to be vilified by those who wish to push them aside and take their place, forgetting the Russian proverb 'What you sow, that shall you reap!' or 'don't dig a pit for someone else, because you will fall into it yourself!'. But the problem lies not in the fact that someone may be upset that he could have been sidelined, because in most cases these people, perhaps after diligent and thankless work over many years, can finally rest with a serene and clear conscience, but in the fact that the cause often suffers, since frequently someone unprepared and inexperienced, or sometimes even worse, takes the place of the person who has left.

Going back a little, I had in mind the psychosis that seized large numbers of the Russian people during the revolution, when the people, propagandised by a small number of agitators, lost their reason. In this abnormal state some said things which subsequently they regretted – but it was then too late.

As for our guilt before our homeland, my modest opinion is that the greater part of that guilt and responsibility lies on the émigré community, since we, in freedom and constrained by no one, are duty-bound to think and act more in national terms. More love, sacrifice, tolerance and mutual understanding are needed.

Enough of philosophical reflections; I leave them to those who are cleverer than me. My task is to describe my life, and the course taken by my life. I shall go on.

So, the White Army in the south of Russia, or rather its remnants, was cast onto the Black Sea.

Anything that would float and could be found at that time in the Black Sea ports was loaded with people. Far from all who wished to leave their motherland were able to get onto something which floated. Many were left behind. Grief was in every heart.

> *No songs were heard on the deck,*
> *the vast sea murmurs,*
> *our native shore is far away,*
> *the memory weighs on the heart.*

I too, a boy of 18, was oppressed by the same sad thoughts. I made my way to the stern of the ship, wishing to keep my 'native shore' in sight as long as possible. When it finally faded from sight, I shed involuntary tears and my heart ached from anguish and grief. Taking from my pocket one of the bottles of wine given to me by the drunken passer-by in Yalta, I opened it and drowned my grief in wine.

A new epic began in the open sea. From the very first days the haste and unpreparedness of the evacuation began to tell. There had not been sufficient time for preparations. The catastrophe had arrived suddenly, at least for the troops and the junior officers in the army. Immediately, during the first days' sailing, the unpreparedness began to show in the shortage of food and fresh water and also in overloading of the vessel. By the way, our steamer *Crimea*, (renamed from the former 'St. Nicholas Transport' a freighter, the tonnage I don't remember) could accommodate about a thousand men according to the captain. There were more than six thousand in her. Moreover a motorised detachment had been embarked, the vehicles being carried on one side of the deck. The whole steamer listed to the side where the vehicles were loaded. When we were already at sea, when the vessel began to roll, we had to manhandle some of them to the other side. People were packed in like sardines in a tin. Those who were accommodated in the holds were in the better conditions: it was warmer and they were less affected by the motion. Those who were on deck froze and could not always manage to shelter from the wind and rain.

Supplies of food and water soon ran short. We made 'Poltava galushki' out of the flour we had, adding a lion's share of sea-water to make up for the lack of fresh water, thus going some way towards satisfying our hunger. People began to suffer from stomach upsets, so the latrines set up on the ship's sides were always full and queues formed beside them. Everyone waited impatiently for the end of the voyage. Finally the steamer arrived at the Golden Horn and dropped anchor among a huge mass of our various steamships with our companions in distress.

We did not know what our fate would be; there were various rumours and nothing more. Everyone was afraid that we might be handed over to the Soviets. Britain, our former 'ally', had rejected us; hope was still fixed on France. The food situation was bad: we were issued with one Turkish loaf, *Oko*– a bit more than a kilogram for ten men – a little tinned food and something, I don't remember what, from the kitchen. Lighters brought drinking water. The ship was encircled by small boats with traders of various kinds, mainly dealing in foodstuffs – bread, some dried fruits and tobacco. The prices were unbelievable: for a gold ring one was hard pressed to get a loaf of bread and a bunch of dried figs. Hungry people would give anything they had to do something to satisfy their hunger.

Personally I had nothing: my entire baggage consisted of a set of underwear and a spare pair of trousers (since mine were in poor shape), a rifle, a sabre and a saddle. In my pocket I had several thousand roubles issued by our government in southern Russia which were no use to anyone. So I had to make do with what we were given. Moreover we were to spend three weeks in quarantine. Our situation was bad, but most of us kept up our spirits, hoping for better things to come.

Finally our situation became clear: we were to be sent to a small town in the Dardanelles, Gallipoli, where the infantry and cavalry regiments of the remnants of our army were to be stationed. The quarantine period had come to an end and our steamer, with the others, set sail. Not long afterwards we reached our destination. Gallipoli was a small town which had suffered greatly during the war. Hence most of the buildings were in a wretched condition and the problem of quarters was critical.

Our regiment was quartered right on the sea shore, close to the jetty – under the open sky on wet ground, bearing in mind that it was the beginning of December i.e. of winter. Although here winter brought none of our (Russian) frosts, there was an abundance of rain.

To our joy food supplies improved; there seemed no longer to be a threat that we would be sent back home. Apart from camp fatigues, we found ourselves more and more often detailed to work on unloading and transporting provisions and everything else necessary for the urgent needs of a thousand men of the Army. I write 'Army' since these thousands of men had in fact not yet turned into a mob of refugees or something even worse.

From the very first days of the arrival of army units in Gallipoli, the army commander, Infantry General Kutepov, with all his characteristic energy, began to reorganise the units under his command, trying to turn them into a military force. The General would appear unexpectedly absolutely everywhere and instil proper order, sparing no one. He would punish offenders severely and would encourage and promote those who conducted themselves well. The whole camp became filled with life. Parade ground drill and other exercises began. Order and cleanliness were established everywhere and even the comforts needed in those conditions. Parades and competitions began. Various sporting teams, theatrical troupes and choirs etc. appeared. Our units were often visited by various foreign representatives, who were amazed at the spirit reigning in our units. Our units burned with ardour to take up their mission again. They had had enough already of remaining in one place without any action, but the hour had not yet come. It came much later – exactly twenty years later!

In spring our regiment was moved to a tented camp seven kilometres from the town. The tents were large ones for up to a hundred men. There were also smaller ones for the officers and various services. There was no equipment, so each of us made himself a bed of branches placed on solid poles (fortunately close to the camp there was a forest with plenty of bushes). We used grass for a mattress. The camp was divided into two by a small stream which provided the camp with water for drinking, cooking, and washing clothes. The infantry units and corps headquarters were on one side of the stream and the cavalry units with the cavalry divisional staff on the other.

The infantry division was, I believe, commanded by General Vitkovsky, the cavalry division by General Barbovich. Our regiment was commanded by Colonel Apukhtin (Her Majesty's Life Guards Ulan Regiment). The commander of our training detachment was Captain Erdelli of Her Majesty's Life Guards Cuirassier Regiment.

Captain Erdelli did not long remain our commander. He was a Hungarian national and soon departed for Hungary, the land of his ancestors. (By the way the late first wife of P.P. Levonenko had the maiden name of Erdelli.) A hussar colonel was appointed as our commander. Our course in the training detachment ended in early summer (I don't remember exactly which month), since the programme had been completed and examinations began. When the examinations ended, some of those who had successfully completed the course were promoted to NCO. I turned out to be amongst the first, which helped me to be made troop NCO when a training detachment for scouts was formed.

As time passed, our camp was occasionally visited by General Vrangel, the commander-in-chief, when there was always a parade. The commander-in-chief would always lift our spirits and told us that negotiations for us to move to Balkan countries were well in train. There was a delay because of the death of King Peter the First of Yugoslavia, but King Alexander, who succeeded to the throne, had ordered that everything necessary be prepared to receive units of our cavalry and deploy them to guard the state borders.

The first echelon soon sailed on the Turkish steamer Reshid Pasha; the second echelon, to which our Guards Battalion was assigned, was preparing to sail[10].

When the training detachment course was completed and the unit broken up, our reserve regiment was also broken up. All the members of cavalry regiments of the various colours were assigned to units. All ranks of the 1st and 2nd Guards Divisions[11] were assigned to us: the Chevalier Guards, the Horse Guards, His and Her Majesties' Cuirassiers, the Horse Grenadiers, His and Her Majesties' Life Guards Ulans, the Grodno Hussars and the Horse Guards Artillery.

An independent 'Guards Cavalry Regiment' was formed from the remaining troops of these regiments. Our former regimental commander, Colonel Apukhtin of Her Majesty's Life Guards Ulans, was appointed commander of the regiment. Our unit of Her Majesty's Cuirassiers (my unit) was included in the 3rd squadron; there were three squadrons in total.

When all the guards were finally gathered into one family, there were touching reunions with comrades in arms whom some of us had not seen for a long time!

---

[10] This sentence is boxed, but there is no indication where it should go. (*Trans. Note*)

[11] There were two Imperial Guard Cavalry Divisions in old Russia, each with several regiments. Each regiment was customarily assigned to a royal family member. The White Army seems to have taken over the names of these regiments.

Life in the regiment gradually took on a regular rhythm. We met men we had not known before, both officers and other ranks, and everything fell into normal routine. In the meantime the quartermasters were ordered to see that the reborn guards regiment had a proper appearance for the conditions, as far as that was possible. The possibilities were not the best, but, nevertheless, all ranks in the regiment were issued with white shirts, grey trousers (made from blankets) and forage caps of the proper colours for their regiments. When all the other ranks and the officer corps had been reclothed, a photographer was found and the whole regiment was photographed. Each member of the regiment received a photograph as a souvenir; mine I have kept until now (also enlarged)[12].

In the meantime training kept up a cracking pace. I had in addition an increased workload in training the scout detachment. In expectation of an imminent departure for Yugoslavia, spirits did not droop, but rose with every day. Finally the embarkation date was announced and we began to get ready. Each of us got himself and his few possessions into proper order, putting aside everything unnecessary and packing in a kit-bag only what might be useful in the future.

The day for us to leave the camp finally came and we marched in column to Gallipoli harbour for embarkation. As we passed the memorial to those of our comrades who remained at rest in foreign ground, our regiment gave them a last farewell on the command, 'March to attention – eyes left!'. To the left of the road, a hundred paces away, was the cemetery

---

[12] Appears in the middle of this book and also on the back cover.

where our dead comrades were buried. Among the graves there rose a memorial constructed of many hundreds of stones. The command had ordered every soldier in our corps to bring a stone to where the memorial was being built, taking symbolic part in its construction. A similar memorial, only smaller, was built by the Gallipolians in France in the Russian cemetery there. I still have photographs of both these memorials. Subsequently the memorial at Gallipoli, and the graves, were maintained for a long time by a local resident who received some recompense from the Society of Gallipolians, but during the last earthquake it was so damaged that it could not be restored. So, with a last glance at the memorial, our regiment went on to the harbour to embark on the Turkish steamer *Kirasuk*.

The embarkation went well and we sailed for the Greek port of Salonika.

When we entered the Dardanelles (a narrow strait), our attention was drawn to the shores, which were lined with a great many ships of various kinds, sizes and types – wrecked British ships from the First World War. During that war, Churchill, the British Navy Minister, tried to break through the defences of the Dardanelles in order to force Turkey out of its coalition with Germany, but, as it turned out, the British fleet was almost all destroyed by the Turks. The Turkish defence was led by Kemal Pasha, then still a young officer (a captain if I am not mistaken), later the leader of the rising against the Sultan and, after his overthrow, President of the Turkish Republic.

We arrived safely at the Greek port of Salonika, where we disembarked from the steamer and entrained. Some hours later, crossing the Yugoslav frontier, we arrived at the town of Gevdelija, where we left the train and found ourselves in a large clearing, where the Yugoslav Army had prepared for us a splendid meal. Before the meal each of us was given a loaf of bread weighing one kilogram. Men who had long been starving did not wait for the meal, but started on the bread immediately, finishing off the fresh, tasty bread with great enjoyment before the meal started. Afterwards, when we received our pay, many of us who had been given the bread in the morning ate it for lunch and bought another kilogram of bread for dinner; this went on until we made up for the long period of hunger.

From our first days in Yugoslavia we were assigned to the Yugoslav Border Guard. We were issued with uniforms, rifles and everything proper for the Yugoslav Army, and we began parade drill. This went on for several weeks, until it was found that we had mastered the subtleties. I have omitted to say that we arrived in Yugoslavia in the last days of August, 1921.

When we joined the Border Guard, changes took place with our officers: the soldiers, including all the NCOs, were counted as privates; the junior officers (below squadron commander) as NCOs of the Yugoslav Army. Only the squadron commander had officer status and wore a Russian officer's uniform. Each squadron had assigned to it a Yugoslav officer as commanding officer and a second officer as his aide, a sergeant (Feldwebel) and two junior NCOs. After the end of training and a parade to mark it, we were told that we were being sent to Dalmatia, to the maritime frontier, which soon eventuated.

I describe what happened in our squadron, but in all probability the same thing happened to the other units of our cavalry which had arrived in Yugoslavia with us.

So we entrained and set off for our destination: Dalmatia. The wagons were nothing elegant – goods wagons as usual. However there was room for all; the weather was fine and warm; the landscapes changed constantly, reminiscent of our southern regions. We rejoiced that the period of semi-starvation and uncertainty in Gallipoli was over.

Into the Balkans

We travelled first on a normal gauge, but, when we came to a mountainous region in Bosnia, we transferred to a narrow gauge, and here we began to run into problems! Our train was hauled by a little steam engine which ran on wood. Sometimes, on particularly steep climbs in the hilly region, we had a pusher (a second, similar little engine), and progress was slow. The train climbed so slowly that many of us would get out and walk, on the one hand to stretch after sitting for so long and on the other to lighten the load for the engine. Finally we reached the highest point on the Romanija Mountain before the town of Sarajevo, that same historic city where the Austrian Crown Prince Ferdinand was assassinated, setting off the First World War, and began the descent towards the city of Dubrovnik. That name is purely Croatian: earlier in Roman times and under Austrian rule it was called Ragusa. According to historical sources the

Russian Princess Tarakanova,[13] a claimant to the Russian throne, once found refuge there. She was the rival of the reigning Catherine II, who despatched a Russian squadron under Admiral Orlov (one of her favourites) with orders to bring her back to Petersburg, which he did. Princess Tarakanova died in the dungeons of the fortress. The railway did not reach as far as Dubrovnik itself, but only as far as the port of Gruj, where we left the train and were housed close by in modern barracks which had belonged to the Austro-Hungarian Army. Other units in our echelon were housed in the ancient barracks of the fortress of Dubrovnik, where we went in groups to visit our companions in arms and inspect the famous old fortress. We did not stay there long, since soon we began to be sent off by steamer to our posts along the shore and on the nearby islands of the Dalmatian coast.

Our squadron, which was renamed by the Yugoslav command as the 16th Ceta i.e. 16th Company, was allocated the islands Korčula and Mljet, to which we were to be taken by steamship. According to the plan worked out by the command, two companies were to be sent to Korčula, the more populated island, and one company to Mljet.

The 1st Company with all its headquarters staff i.e. our commanding officer and his staff and also the Yugoslav officers and their people (the official commanding officer was the Yugoslav Captain First Class Svetozar Stuparovic), his aide Captain Second Class (I don't recall his name) and the other Yugoslavs made up headquarters, which was

---

[13] Yelizaveta Alekseyevna, 1753 – 1775. Tarakanova is from the Russian 'tarakan' or cockroach..

established in the very centre of the town of Korčula. This was linked with the other towns by steamship lines. I found myself in the 1st Company, but my lot was the very worst post, far away in a deserted part of the island, where there was no one close by. The nearest village was three to four kilometres away. There were two Yugoslavs with me; we were housed in a hayshed visited occasionally by fisherman escaping bad weather.

The 2nd Company, commanded by Lieutenant-Colonel Lenitsky, was located in the towns of Blato (the headquarters) and Vela Luka (i.e. a small port). The 3rd Company occupied Mljet, under the command of Lieutenant–Colonel Mukhanov.

These islands, like others in the Adriatic Sea, consist mainly of rocky hills covered with conifer forest and bush; here and there in the centre there are quite large areas of fertile ploughed land. The people are industrious; many of them take a great deal of trouble to undermine the large rocks, or simply dig out small ones, reclaiming from nature small plots and planting them with grape vines. The rocks they use to build walls around their plots. This work takes up all their free time.

Their main occupations are the production of wine (and spirits from the unusable leftovers of the grapes i.e. the pressings) and fishing. Some who can plant enough olive trees make olive oil. There are very few families who do not have someone overseas to provide financial help to support and improve their properties. The population is welcoming and hospitable; they belong to the Catholic faith and their moral standards are quite high. Their way of life is patriarchal. All the children have to go to school.

Almost every settlement has its church and school. The inhabitants are organised in cooperatives covering the various spheres of activity. In every settlement there are reading rooms where many spend their leisure, and also inns where one may have a drink and a snack and even get a room for the night. Some churches are popular with tourists, as are other ancient structures, as for example ancient fortresses, villas dating from Roman times (the villa of the Roman Emperor Diocletian in the town of Split and many others in various towns) and other historical sites. Dalmatia abounds in historic structures, has a wonderful climate, magnificent sandy beaches, a welcoming population and excellent wines which are exported to many countries. It is a favourite destination for tourists even from distant America... The seven years I spent in Dalmatia are a very pleasant memory.

I was not long to remain at that deserted and miserable post, since I was replaced by a Serb and sent to another post in quite a big village. There I got to know the local priest and doctor, who were very good and responsive people. I would get from them books to read; although at first I had a poor understanding of what I was reading, nevertheless I made rapid progress in the local Croatian language. There were three men at the post: two Serbs and I. The NCO in charge was an elderly sergeant who had served in the war of 1912-13 against Bulgaria and the war of 1914 against Austro-Hungary. We were housed in a small detached cottage; we took turns to cook; life was no longer tedious (as at the first post) and took a happier and more varied course. Here for the first time in my life I learnt to use oars and often did so, although at first I suffered from blistered hands. In time the skin hardened and I could keep it up for a long time and even compete with the local oarsmen. Our post was five kilometres from headquarters (on foot), but it was closer by sea and I often, with the local inhabitants, used a boat to get to the town where our headquarters were.

As a rule there is no spring water for drinking on the islands, so every householder constructs near the house a capacious concrete tank to collect rainwater from the roof. People and their animals, those who have them, use this water. Cattle are rare. Mainly they have sheep and goats for milk and harness donkeys and mules to transport loads: firewood, rocks and wine in skins. Cattle are brought from the mainland, but these are for the butchers and do not stay long. The local inhabitants tell of an interesting incident with water which had happened a few years before. There was very little rain that year and very little water in the tanks. By Christmas no one had water. They loaded boats with barrels and crossed the sea to the mainland to get fresh water. Filling their barrels, they set off back (it was several kilometres to the mainland; I don't remember exactly how many). When they had got halfway it began to rain heavily, the boats began to fill with water, and they had to empty the water out of the barrels to avoid catastrophe. Imagine their disappointment when they reached the shore near their village, only to learn that not a single drop had fallen there! Christmas dinner was meat cooked in…wine!

Life in the Border Guard was relatively quiet, with no unpleasantness. The end of a year's service was near and there were rumours that, since the

country had made a full transition to a state of peace
(four years had passed since the end of the war and
the unification of Serbs, Croats and Slovenians in one
state), there was no need to retain military units on
the state borders. It was found necessary to replace
them, following the example of the former Austro-
Hungary, with a financial control service (armed) to
co-ordinate operations with the customs and excise
branches of the Ministry of Finance.

So, from the first of November 1922, after
fourteen months on border guard, I with others was
transferred to a new service. Consequently we were
deployed in new places. Our material situation was
immediately improved (our pay became three times
more than it had been!). I and three other comrades
were sent to another island, Vis, with a small town of
the same name. At the other end of the island there
was another small town, Komiža; there was a similar
detachment there, to which three of our comrades
were sent. In our detachment, apart from the NCO in
charge, there were two Yugoslavs who had been long
in the service and whose experience gradually passed
to us. My Russian comrades: S.F. Kuryatenko, an
elderly (about fifty) former second-lieutenant of Her
Majesty Mariya Fedorovna's Life Guards Cuirassier
Regiment, M.I. Kurenin, and a volunteer, I.S. Kozlov
(a former prisoner of war from the Red Army).

These were the men whom fate had brought
together with me in this new place. Unfortunately,
our commander, a Croat who had been in this service
under the Austrian government, from the very first
days was not very generous in his attitude toward us,
so that a covert tension soon began to be felt between
us. As time went on we became more convinced of

our commander's unfriendly attitude and looked for a way of getting rid of him. We were aware that he would often take bribes, but we had no documentary evidence. However powerful our complaints, they were against our own commander and of course could not be accepted, the more so since he had friends even at the highest level.

Despite our efforts to seek a convenient opportunity, we failed for a long time to do so. In addition, there was no unanimity amongst us, since Kuryatenko was attached to the head of customs and was responsible directly to him; an intelligent young man, good-natured and fully content. Kozlov, perhaps despite his own wishes, turned out seemingly to be the favourite of the commander, who often made use of him for services of a private nature which had nothing to do with the service, and hence protected him. So, perhaps even following the Jesuit principle – divide and rule, the commander disliked Kurenin and me and would often give us the worst and the most onerous jobs.

For some reason, there came from the centre an order to carry out an immediate inventory of tobacco products in the outlets of local traders, of which there were three, one of them possessing a store from which he distributed to the other two retail traders, while also having a retail outlet himself. The inventory was in connection with an increase in prices, and the difference on the existing stock had to be taken accordingly from the trader, accounted for and paid to the local tax office. Kurenin and I were allocated one each of the retail traders, while the wholesale trader was to be checked by the commander himself for both his wholesale and retail outlets. Knowing our commander's methods, we resolved to check his work, in the hope of discovering some abuse of his authority. This was to see whether the totals corresponded or not. This was to do with the inventory recorded by the commander. Our inventories were a somewhat simpler matter, since each of us kept copies of his inventory and all we had to do was to collect the sums designated by the commander. But we were lucky at the outset. The commander would always tear his rough copies in half and throw them in a basket, which was emptied every morning by a servant and the papers burnt. Here we kept watch and offered to burn the papers ourselves, first looking through them carefully and fortunately finding what we needed. We had copies of the inventories which we had compiled. When we checked them against our own copies, we saw that the commander had reduced the sums when he copied them out.

The statements compiled by the commander contained, along with the original inventory, a new set of figures which appeared in the statements concerning payments to the state of the difference in price. It was these inventory sheets with double sets of figures which we found in the basket. So we had achieved our aim of discovering documents indicating abuse. We compiled an action plan and set a date on which we intended to make a brief statement to the head of the district group and ask him to look at the matter, in reality to investigate. On the date we had set, however, I was sent out with Kozlov on patrol for 36 hours. Kozlov had not been told of our enterprise, nor did we know whether he had guessed what we were doing. I don't know exactly how it happened, but, when we returned from the patrol, the commander already knew what we were up to. This we were told by Kurenin, who met us when we arrived at the town. When we reached our quarters, we had to unload our carbines, put them in the rack, and then clean up and have supper, since it was already evening. Now something happened which to a large extent spoilt our plans, and we nearly found ourselves in the dock! As we came into our quarters, I quickly removed the cartridge clip from the magazine and put it in a bag. The carbine with bolt withdrawn I placed in the rack and then went off to wash before supper. While I was washing, there was a shot. Everyone in the building rushed to the room where the shot had been heard.

In the middle of the room stood a distraught Kozlov. When he was asked what had happened he mumbled that he had forgotten to take a cartridge out of the magazine and had pulled the trigger! Whether this was carelessness or something worse has remained a mystery to the present day. The neighbours came running when they heard the shot (we were on the first floor, with the district court below) with an officer of the court who lived with his family on the court premises. Alarmed, they started to ask what had happened. Our commander was first to say that it was nothing in particular, that he had forgotten to take out a cartridge and pulled the trigger. Those present were satisfied by this reply and dispersed.

The night passed without incident, but in the morning our commander came to the office, called us in and tried to persuade us to cover up everything that had happened with his falsification. Before he arrived, friends in the gendarmerie station had already told us that our commander had been there to ask their chief to arrest one of us, who it was they did not know, but their chief had replied that he could only do that when ordered to by his superior officer. Perhaps for that reason we were not arrested, our commander changed his plans and tried to come to terms with us, reckoning that, when everything quietened down, he would try to get rid of us. We, however, being aware after our past disagreements with him that he would not keep his word, rejected his proposal. Moreover, he had already started rumours that we had tried to kill him, indeed that it was not Kozlov, but Kurenin who had fired the shot, and he had knocked the carbine away and the bullet had gone into to the air.

The next day our district chief arrived with our Russian colonel, who was attached to him, and an investigation began. From the very first day our commander was stood aside and someone else appointed to his post temporarily. We, on the other hand, continued to carry out our duties as before. The investigation went on for about a week and a half, and those who were conducting it became convinced of our innocence. The record of investigation went up official channels to the Procurator-General, who found that the charge against us of attempting to murder the commander was unfounded, i.e. false, and accused him of falsifying evidence in his official capacity (on the increase in excise) and of falsely accusing us of making an attempt on his life. There soon followed a jury trial, which, taking into account his long service and family situation, did not find him guilty. However, a disciplinary court in the service pronounced sentence that our commander could not in the future be appointed to responsible positions or be promoted. Kurenin and I were transferred to separate detachments in different towns. So ended the story of the excise increase and the shot into the ceiling.

So Kurenin was transferred to the town of Jelsa on the island of Hvar and I to the town of Stari Grad (the Old City) on the same island. The distance between these towns was about 9-10 kilometres overland; there was a steamer twice a week. My friend from the same class in the gymnasium, Ivan Gavrilovich Udovitsky, was posted in Stari Grad, so we had a good time together. While I was in Stari Grad, I do not recall how, we came to know that in Belgrade courses had started up (for those who had not completed Gymnasium in Russia) for the leaving certificate. We asked our Colonel Mukhanov to help us enrol for these courses. Colonel Mukhanov, instead of encouraging and helping us, began to dissuade us, saying that we would have to sit an entrance examination, which would be hard after an interval of 2 to 3 years, and even if we were successful in the examination not everyone would manage to get a grant to enter university. This reply discouraged us and we were not game to leave the service. Much later we discovered that everyone who wished to was accepted and received a grant, not only for the courses, but also to continue their education at the university. It was, however, already too late and we had missed our one opportunity to continue our education. In Stari Grad my life was very good and happy. Udovitsky and I developed good friends amongst the locals, who were very friendly towards us, particularly the local 'elite': the civil servants, traders, even the clergy (Catholic priests – there were no other religions). We sang in the local choir, not only secular songs, but sometimes also religious, and always at funerals. Udovitsky acted in the local drama society, where he had great success (particularly amongst the ladies).

We were both members of the local society of civil servants and other intelligentsia, which met periodically in the local restaurant to spend the whole night in a pleasant atmosphere. There were amusing incidents with those who went over the mark in the consumption of wine, which was supplied abundantly by the wine merchant, an unfailing participant in our meetings. Early in the morning those of us who stood more firmly on our legs accompanied those who were weaker to their homes, and ourselves took our swimming costumes, went out of town and settled down to sleep at the edge of the forest by the sea shore. When dinner-time approached, we would bathe and set off home. Once two of my comrades and I set off in a boat along the coast and, having covered ten kilometres or so, decided to bathe and rest. It was spring and the sun was warm. Preoccupied, we forgot that this was our first swim that year and got so burnt that we found it very hard to pull the oars. Next time we were more careful. I spent two years in Stari Grad and was once again transferred to the island of Vis, but to the other end, to the town of Komiža, which I mentioned above. In Komiža there were also two Russians; the commander was very good-natured and the work was easy. We would often sail with fishermen to a tiny island where there were the best vineyards in Dalmatia.

So I came to spend time at two posts, but, when a new post was opened quite close (about two kilometres) to my old friend, Kurenin, I was transferred to it and we were able to meet often to recall our adventures. My new commander, like Kurenin's, turned out to be very good-natured. They treated us well and we repaid them in the same coin, often helping them to carry out their administrative duties, which were not hard for us, since we already spoke the local language well and moreover we were studying hard for examinations for promotion in the service, thus broadening our horizons. When we had completed the whole preparatory course, we applied to be admitted to the examinations. At the same time we applied for Yugoslav citizenship, in accordance with King Alexander's decree that Russians, in order to improve their situation, could take up Yugoslav citizenship, which would not be a hindrance if the time came for them to return to their homeland, freed from Bolshevism. We passed the examinations and were registered as candidates for higher rank and permanency. This was in early 1927. It was our bad luck that a new budget brought staffing cuts and, although we were not included in the cuts, rumour had it that similar cuts were planned for 1928. Our spirits fell. We expected the worst, since our commander's recommendation that we be given permanency and promotion was held up at the last stage (in the Regional Inspectorate). This circumstance disheartened us, and we waited for the new budget in the next year, 1 April 1928.

In March we had news that…

[Pages 29 -30 are missing. *Trans. note*]

...this was not the first incident and that a search was being made for him to bring him to trial for many of his misdemeanours.

I had to come to terms with my bad luck and forget about it, but be more careful in the future. In order to keep the savings I had left, I looked for whatever work I could find and at one time helped a Russian acquaintance in his vegetable and fruit business, but he himself was not doing wonderfully well and, as winter approached, trade got worse. One of my comrades whom I had met in Simferopol while in the training detachment offered to find me work in the firm in which he worked as receiver of monies, which I accepted. However, knowing from experience that in winter a receiver's income was paltry, since they received a percentage of the sums they collected, my friend advised me to enrol for fitters' courses, which had existed for 7 years in the town of Kruševac at the Military Engineering Factory. At the end of the courses one was guaranteed work at the same factory. My friend was already enrolled for these courses, so he helped to do the same. The courses began on 1 January, 1929. There was a month or so to go until then.

When the time was near, we put in order our petty affairs and received from the State Commission where we worked (in administration) our Russian documents, travel allowance and other sums. We presented ourselves in time – in the last days of December, 1928 – at the departure point in the Russian House, where the State Commission was. On the same day we took the train and by evening we were in Kruševac (about 100 kilometres from Belgrade). In Kruševac we were expected and taken to barracks belonging to the Military Engineering Factory, where a huge hall had been prepared for us with beds and everything else necessary. More than thirty of us arrived for the courses.

A few words about Kruševac[14] itself and the factory where we were to take the training course and then work. Kruševac was a small provincial town with a population of 50-60,000. In the nineteenth century it had been the capital of Serbia in the reign of King Milan Obrenovic. His residence remains there to this day; a relatively small single-storey villa. There was also a small-arms factory serving the army of the time. After the war of 1914-1918, when the Austro-Hungarian Empire collapsed and out of it came the union of Serbs, Croats and Slovenes, a large factory was built in Kruševac where 15-18,000 workers were employed and which had a number of divisions: artillery, machine-gun, rifle, pyrotechnics etc. Unfortunately the town and factory were greatly handicapped by the absence of a river; supplying water was difficult. Eventually water was brought from a reservoir constructed several kilometres from the town, but that is not the same as a permanent, living river.

So we were in Kruševac. Next day we met the administration and teaching staff of our courses. The course head and mathematics teacher was Lieutenant-General (of artillery) Gorelov (Russian army ranks) the secretary Colonel Danilov, and the teachers;

---

[14] The author names the town in Russian as 'Krashchevets' but Kruševac best fits the description. (*Trans.note*)

electrics – Colonel of Artillery A.I. Degtyarev: physics – Major-General N. Chuykevich; machine parts – engineer F. Gladkov; steam boilers – engineer Zhemchuzhnikov; resistance of materials – engineer Sachkov; manual operations – engineer B. Fedorov; army chief of supply – Colonel S.P. Chuykevich. On the factory side: Director Yugoslav General of Division Terzibašič; Lieutenant-Colonel Varant; two other officers whose names I do not remember; and two master tradesmen instructors in manual operations.

In their organization, the founders of the courses aimed to provide their pupils with skills corresponding to those of assistant engineers. The programme was worked out with this in mind; hence only those who had completed not less than six classes of secondary school were admitted.

After the meeting with the staff, training began immediately. Every morning there was timetabled theoretical training, with practical in the afternoon. Classes were from eight till twelve with a one-hour break for dinner and then from one till five – six days a week: a total of forty-eight hours. Time passed rapidly. Everyone worked fast to complete the course and get the best training, so that when jobs were allocated he would get the best possible placement, where he would have the opportunity to develop and broaden as well and widely as possible his skill in the area.

After six months examinations began. The examination commission, apart from some of our instructors, included three officers of the Yugoslav army, two senior tradesmen and two junior tradesmen. They lasted a whole week. When they ended and results were announced, job placements began. Those who had expressed a wish to leave and find work independently were not compelled to stay, but there were very few and they were the exception. Examination results were taken into account in job placement. Those with the best results were allocated to jobs where they could continue to develop their skills. I succeeded in getting one of the best placements – to perfect my skills on universal lathes, where I often had to do calculations. The workshop in which I was placed had been set up recently and equipped with new, modern machines received from Germany as 'reparations'. It produced various machine tools for the manufacture of parts for rifles, machine-guns etc. Sometimes it made parts for various machines when they wore out and needed repair or replacement.

Finding love and family

Once I was established at work, I decided to acquire a family. I was twenty-eight. It was not easy for a Russian migrant to find a bride, particularly if he had some of his own requirements, and I had some. I had to find girls to my taste and who would find me likeable, but their relatives often intervened: why do you need a Russian when there are plenty of our own who are just as good and perhaps even better? One fine day your Russian will go off home to Russia, and what will happen to you then?! But where there is God's will, there is always a way. For some reason the subject of marriage came up in a conversation in the family of a Kuban Cossack who was married to a Bulgarian. They asked me why I did not get married.

I described to them frankly my situation, my views on marriage, my requirements of a future bride, my views on the family, the preservation of pure morals in the family etc. The Cossack's wife responded that she knew a girl of that kind, but I had met her several years before, when she was still at school – perhaps she had changed since? In a nutshell, they undertook to write to this girl to ask her to call on them when she was in our town; she occasionally came to our town with her sister or her sister's sister-in-law, who, as a teacher, would often visit.

It was December of 1931, there was deep snow, and suddenly in the evening the Bulgarian came running to where I lived, saying, 'Come with me quickly; the girl I told you about is at my house!'

I got ready quickly and went over. We met and somehow found a common language straight way; her sincerity, her pure and open face, a total absence of the least slyness, pride or anything else off-putting – we seemed to have known each other for ages. We agreed that at Christmas I would visit her sister and brother-in-law; he was a teacher 28 kilometres from Kruševac, where I lived. When, an hour later, we met her brother-in-law and said that we had agreed to meet at his house for Christmas, he promised to come before the holidays and make arrangements. But the holidays passed and our meeting did not take place!

As I later discovered, the brother-in-law was against our getting to know each other. Briefly, he took the attitude that we have plenty of our own and suggested to her his own friends, whom his sister-in-law disliked. I thought myself offended by the tactlessness of the brother-in-law, who had promised to come before the holidays and did not, but the girl was also displeased and wrote about it to the Bulgarian, since she disagreed with her brother-in-law. When I learnt what had happened, I went to see the girl to meet her mother and with the firm intention of asking for her hand. This was obviously the girl destined for me, since I straight away found a common language with her mother. This was my wife today Slava!

It was the middle of Lent and we agreed to get engaged at Easter and prepare for the wedding, which we set for Holy Trinity. We set about preparing for our new life enthusiastically and, despite some difficulties and obstacles, we managed everything. We had problems with somewhere to live, but we were promised a flat in the factory workers' settlement.

In the meantime a Serbian friend agreed to let us have a room he had vacant until we got the government flat. The Serbian custom is that at the wedding the young couple are accompanied by two witnesses (they do not have groomsmen). (The crowns are placed directly on the heads; no one holds them). The first godfather stands behind the groom. He has the duty of christening (in the future) all the children and also presiding at their wedding. Hence he is held in great esteem. After the godfather's death, this falls to his eldest son. The second godfather stands behind the bride and is also much esteemed by the couple.

The Russian engineer-colonel of artillery A.I. Degtyarev, whom I have mentioned above, agreed to be godfather, and the former Austrian colonel Stanko Turudija, a Bosnian, to stand as second godfather.

Colonel Stanko Turudija, a Bosnian by origin was an interesting man. He was short, perhaps one centimetre taller than Stojanovič, just as thin, with lively eyes which quickly lit up when he began to reminisce about his victories on the Italian front during the First World War, when he was known as 'the fiery major'! He was, despite his position as an Austrian officer, a Slav by nature and, leading his Bosnian soldiers into battle, he would always inspire them by saying,

'Do not forget that it is not a foreign land which you are defending, but your own. Do not allow an enemy boot to tread it and oppress your parents, wives, mothers and children!'

Always going before his troops in attack, he emphasised his readiness to be the first to take the enemy's blows. His soldiers, Bosnians known for their courage, were inspired by the bravery of their commander.

One of his greatest victories was the battle of Caporetto, in which, just before the end of the war, the Italian forces advanced rapidly and resolutely, driving before them the demoralised Austrian troops, to seize as much as possible of Austrian territory, which was inhabited by Slovenes and Croats. It was here at Caporetto that the destiny of this part of Slav territory was decided. The Bosnian counter-attack, led by Colonel S. Turudija, was so vigorous that the Italians broke and ran in panic, taking with them the units on their flanks. This victory decided the fate of the Slavs, since peace was soon concluded and the Serbs, Croats and Slovenes were united in a single state. This is a brief description of the personality of Colonel Turudija, who, following the unification after the end of the First World War, was commissioned as colonel in the Yugoslav Army and served in it for some time before retiring.

At a meeting of relatives and godparents it was decided that the wedding would be on the first day of Holy Trinity, since that was most convenient for all. The senior priest himself (the church also had three junior priests) promised to marry us between matins and mass in the Kruševac cathedral. The wedding breakfast was to be in the living-room of our temporary host. In view of the limited situation, at the reception (i.e the breakfast) there were only relatives and close friends. So my dream of many years was fulfilled: I had started a family.

Some months after the wedding we managed to get a flat in the factory workers' settlement and the question of where to live was resolved. Our life passed pleasantly, but pleasure is always mixed with grief and we soon were to suffer a great misfortune which almost ended in tragedy.

Car crash

We had introduced a young friend of ours, a shopkeeper, to a young lady from the same town as my wife, and we arranged to go to the engagement. We went by car and, after a successful outing, were returning home in the evening. The driver was rather drunk and, quite close to Kruševac, drove the car into a ditch. The car was at an angle of 45 degrees in the ditch. My wife and another woman in the car were frightened, my wife particularly, and started screaming. People arriving at the scene got everyone out of the car and helped to drag it back onto the road. The driver started the motor and we reached home. During the night my wife experienced severe pain in the abdomen (she was three months pregnant) and blood appeared. Next day I went to work, hoping that everything would return to normal, but, when I got back home, my wife told me that the pain was no less and the bleeding would not stop. In the following days she told me that she was better (hiding the truth because she was afraid that a doctor might intervene).

We wrote to her mother in Kraljevo, who came and took care of her sick daughter, continuing to conceal that there was no improvement; on the contrary things were getting worse. It was already the second week. We called in the doctor, who advised an operation, but my wife would not accept that, and the doctor attempted to stop the bleeding with injections. However nothing helped and in the third week he stated categorically: it was either an operation or he could not guarantee her life. He wanted to send her to hospital immediately, which she refused. I was called from work urgently so that a joint decision could be made on what to do.

My wife absolutely refused to go to hospital. The doctor said that an operation in hospital would be free, since he would do it on the insurance. If we wanted it in his private surgery it would be expensive; he named a sum equal to two-thirds of my monthly pay! When I said that I did not have the sum in cash and would pay him in instalments, he refused. After that I turned to my lawyer, who was looking after my claim from a debtor for twice that sum, and he persuaded the doctor to postpone payment.

After the operation, I asked the doctor whether my wife would be able to have children in the future. The doctor replied that we should forget about children for a few years (2-3 years), since my wife was in poor health and needed to recover and build up her strength. What for another strong woman would be easy, for her could be fatal. Discovering that she came from Kraljevo, where there are two rivers, one of which in its upper course had resorts with curative springs, he advised us to move there and bathe frequently in the river. Close to Kraljevo, one kilometre from the town and right on the river, my wife had a small block of land (about one hectare), which was very convenient.

Kraljevo

Taking the doctor's advice, I began to arrange a transfer to Kraljevo, to the aircraft factory there. On the one hand I had to have the consent of the director of the Kraljevo factory; a Russian who had long worked in that factory and had good relations with the director took that on. On the other hand I had to get my own director to give me permission in writing, which was required by the factory director in Kraljevo.

When I applied to my own director, he refused his consent. Directors were generally unwilling to let good and reliable workers go (I counted as one of these), and I was not game to resign independently, because it could happen that I would not be accepted at Kraljevo, since there was an agreement between the two factories' administrations not to entice workers from one another. Both factories were state enterprises. Here luck was on my side. My own director went off on a long business trip (several months) and I applied to his deputy, who did not know that my former director had refused, and who gave his consent.

So, in early 1936, I went to work in Kraljevo at the aircraft factory. There was at that time a temporary stoppage at the factory, since work was coming to an end on making spare parts for and maintaining old aircraft of the French type Brege, and the factory was impatiently awaiting an order for twin-engined bombers of the German type Dornier. In addition the factory, which was run by the Ministry of Aviation, was being transferred to a company in which 51% of the shares would be held by the government and 49% by private capital. Also salaries and wages were going up significantly (almost doubling!). Feverish preparations began for the changeover to the new order. Everyone was in a hurry, driven by the thought that our material situation would be much improved. I was lucky to get a government flat belonging to the factory five minutes walk from the very workshop in which I worked on milling machines. The flat was on the first floor (the houses were two-storey) with modern conveniences, at least for the time.

Preparations were soon finished and our directors changed into civilian clothes (the officers amongst the engineers); our pay almost doubled immediately and work started in earnest. Evidently someone at the top knew of the war that was coming and hence increased the pace: it was 1938. We worked ten hours a day (two hours overtime), eight hours on

Saturdays and often four hours on Sundays. 'Life has got better, life has got happier!'

At the same time as our material situation improved, things got worse with rest and recreation. Before this time of abundance my wife and I spent our time out of doors, swimming in summer and on excursions on Sundays and holidays. We became members of the Serbian Choir, which, apart from taking part in church services, had a good repertoire of secular songs. Apart from performances in our town, it often did concerts in other towns.

We sometimes visited newly opened churches (or refurbished), always accompanied by Bishop Nikolaj, a highly educated man (Higher Theological Academy in Russia and in England) and much respected and esteemed in Serbia. When the local Russian priest, the former precentor of the Serbian Choir, was displaced by a Bulgarian, he offered his services (free) to us (the Russian colony), if sufficient voices could be found for the choir. There were enough volunteers, so my wife and I found ourselves in the Russian Choir, periodically singing in the local Serbian church. While we were still in Kruševac my wife and I took part in a group arranging to set up a Russian Club (we still even have a photograph of that group) and were active in the work of the Club, and even took part in the Congress at Zagreb (Yugoslavia).

Our Club President was General Aleksinsky, who, commanding a division sent by the Russian government, took part in the Serbian army's break-through on the Salonika front (Greece) under the command of the then heir to the throne, Prince Alexander. The Club Mentor was Colonel A. I. Degtyarev. I had the position of secretary to the

Mentor. A.I. Degtyarev, who took a room in the house which we rented, which continued until we left for Kraljevo. When we left Kruševac we found a young, newly married Russian couple who took over our former flat; hence our godfather (we regarded him as a father) was guaranteed the assistance he needed, since he was often ill with his liver. We parted with him as with a member of the family and he promised to visit us when he came for treatment to one of the resorts close to Kraljevo.

Pregnant

Once I had moved to Kraljevo to work, my wife and I joined in the work of the local Russian club, a close, active and friendly family. In the meantime my wife had quite recovered. The local climate, bathing in the river Ibar, where the curative springs were, the environment and all the rest had a very beneficial influence on her health and she soon felt she was to be a mother. With great reverence and prayers we awaited the approach of the birth, still taking part in the church choir. According to our calculations, we expected the birth to be about the second week of December and we prepared for that date.

To go back a little, I want to mention a fine and very interesting tradition of the Serbs: the so-called *Krsna Slava*. In Serbia every *Rod* (family) has its heavenly patron, which passes from family to family in the male line. The trouble comes when the male line comes to an end. This was the case with my wife. In her childhood she lost her only brother and had only an elder sister, married to a Serb, a teacher, who had his own *Slava*. Her sister, however, took it on herself to retain their *Slava* Saint Stevan Dečanski, who was regarded as *Velika (Greater) Slava*. However their family had also a lesser *Slava*, Saint Savva, whom their family had taken on someone's advice, so that in their family male children should prevail (i.e. should not die – as had happened earlier), and my wife and her mother retained this *Slava*. When I, my wife and her mother were discussing all the issues connected with the future arrangements in our life, my wife's mother asked me to permit her daughter to continue, in even the most modest way, the memory of her *Slava*, to which I agreed, emphasing that I had great respect for their custom and would myself take part.

This, however, referred to the lesser *Slava* of Saint Savva, while the *Slava* of Saint Mrata (which is the name they gave to the *Slava* of Saint Stevan Dečanski) was not discussed, since her sister retained the latter.

However, Saint Mrata's day was near and my wife's mother was preparing the dough to bake the *kolač* (the name the Serbs give to special bread baked from a sweet dough and topped with communion wafers). 'What if ,' she said to her daughter, 'the *rusich* (i.e. the Russian baby boy) arrives on the *Slava*? She was hoping for a grandson, since her elder daughter had two girls, to carry on their tradition of the *Slava*.

My wife reminded her that there were still two weeks to go, to which her mother replied that that was unimportant; anything is possible.

It was a working day and I was at work. After work and collecting my half-monthly pay, I set off home. In the evening, as I approached the house, it was obvious that there were people rushing about in

71

our flat, which seemed to me very strange. Before I got into the flat, I was met by my mother-in-law, who, worried but with gladness in her eyes, told me that the birth had started and the midwife was with my wife. After an interval, we heard a baby cry, the door opened and the midwife appeared in the doorway carrying the baby, saying that we had a son. Our joy was great, particularly that of my mother-in-law, since she wanted very much a grandson. All of us felt joy in our own way.

Alexander

A few days later our son was christened Alexander. In the first place, he was born on 23 November, 1939, new style; in the old style that day was the festival of Prince Alexander Nevsky[15]. In the second place, godfather at his christening was to be our own godfather Aleksandr Ivanovich Degtyarev, who had agreed to do so while travelling for treatment at one of the resorts close to Kraljevo; he would stop and spend the night with us on his way. However, to our deep regret, A.I. Degtyarev had been buried in Kruševac three weeks before our son was born. My wife and I, summoned by telegram, were at the funeral. He was buried with full military honours; the coffin was borne on a gun carriage with a proper military escort. Almost the whole of the Russian colony came to farewell the deceased, with many members of the Yugoslav army, headed by the director of the factory and the commander of the

---

[15] Russia remained on the Julian calendar until 1918 (when 1 February became 14 February).

artillery regiment stationed there. It was thus that the late King Alexander of Yugoslavia had decreed that Russian officers should be buried.

Now some details about the birth of our son.

First, the question arises why our son had to be born on the eve of the Slava, at seven in the evening on 23 November (Slava was on the 24 November), when, according to our calculations, he should have been born two weeks later. Even today, 37 years later[16], we regard this circumstance as as indication from God that that day should be respected, if not as the day of Slava, then as the day of our son's birth!

Second, the Serbian custom is that after the birth of a child someone from the family or friends goes to the priest and asks for a prayer to be said for the newborn, and for holy water to sprinkle on the newborn. My late mother-in-law, since 24 November was the day of the Slava of Saint Mrata, had the day before, 23 November, baked the kolač which I mentioned above. She took the vessel for the holy water and early in the morning hurried to the church to have the kolač blessed and get the holy water. She arrived at the church very early, when there was no one there except the caretaker, sat on a bench to wait for the priest and dozed off. She awoke when she heard steps approaching, looked up and saw close by Bishop Nikolaj, whom I mentioned above, and ran to him for his blessing. He blessed her and asked, 'What are you looking for here so early, woman?'

My mother-in-law was a loquacious woman, very sociable, quick-witted and bold. She related the whole story to the Bishop: how her daughter in the first year

---

[16] Indicating this part of the manuscript was written in 1976.

of marriage had an accident and lost a child, was ill for a long time, but now on the eve of the Slava had borne a son, that her son-in-law was Russian and that he respects the Slava, and that she had brought the kolač to be blessed and to get a prayer and holy water for the child.

When he heard the story, the Bishop said, 'This is not an ordinary birth, but a sign from God'. He ordered that everything necessary should be prepared for this ceremony in the church, which was all done in his presence.

My mother-in-law was beside herself with joy. As if on wings, she hurried home to share her joy. This ceremony is normally held in the building next to the church, but for her the Bishop himself had ordered that it be in the church! A few days later we christened our son.

Our godfather was a Serb, engineer Mijodrag Naumovič, but only according to our custom, since the Serbian custom is that the godfather himself names the child and his wish is incontestable, which sometimes displeases the parents. Our godfather, however, aware of the Russian custom, found out our wishes from the midwife and replied 'Alexander' when asked for a name by the priest.

Belgrade bombed

With the birth of our son, we began a new purposeful, happy life, since we both loved children and wished to have them. My wife and I gave all our attention and love to the child and my wife's mother competed with us, trying to outdo us in everything.

74

Of course there was war in Europe, which gradually spread.

In Yugoslavia we heard persistent rumours that it was coming close to us. There were diplomatic negotiations. Public opinion in Yugoslavia was divided into two camps; one was for isolation and neutrality; the other asserted that we would not be able to be neutral, since Germany was demanding transit for its armies to Greece and further on to Africa, where a landing of German troops was already planned against the British colonies. 1940 passed with alarms, but uneventfully for us. My wife and I dreamt of building our own house; a block of land for the house had been bought, almost in the very centre of the town (near the railway station); we had collected building materials and intended to sell a block of agricultural land near the river, the proceeds of which would cover the cost of building. We were saving for fittings out of my pay, which was very generous. This was the situation as 1941 arrived.

January and February passed quietly. Lent came and went and everyone awaited a joyous Easter. But man proposes and God disposes! On the day of greatest joy for a Christian, the first day of the Resurrection of Christ, the radio reported early in the morning a raid by German bombers on Belgrade, the capital of Yugoslavia. The bombs had fallen mainly on the city centre, causing great destruction and many casualties.

General Alexander Kutepov (1882-1930), the commander in the Volunteer Army from January 1919 to September 1920. He was kidnapped, and presumably killed, in Paris in 1930 by the OGPU (part of the Russian secret service) posing as French police.

Baron Pyotr Nikolayevich Vrangel (1878-1928). The last
Commander-in-Chief of the White Army, he organised a mass
evacuation across the Black Sea. He published his own memoirs
'Notes' shortly before his death.

Tsarina Mariya Feodorovna (1847-1928), Dowager Empress,
aunt of King George V, fled to London via the Black Sea in 1919.
She sent Christmas cards to members of her life-guard until her
death.

At Gallipoli.
Seventh from
left, front row.

Detail – Efimij in
front and centre.

HMS Tiger at anchor, 1916–17. She was a steamer launched in 1913 and was the most heavily armoured ship in England's navy on entry into WWI. When she ferried Efimij she was considered to be a comparatively old vessel.

In July 1932, Efimij married Slava Melentjevna
Milovanovič.

The back of Efimij's German issued pass.

Потпис имаоца књижице. — Potpis imaoca knjižice.
Podpis lastnika knjižice.

Photo and signature inside a pass, at age 39, shortly before
the birth of his only son.

The symbol of the Russian Liberation Army,
(Русская освободительная армия), part of Hitler's military
machine. The Serbian-based Russian Corps and other white
Russian units, were forced to become part of the Wehrmacht
towards the end of the War (1944).

The symbol adopted by Russian Corps (Русский корпус)
veterans after WWII.

Family snaps.

The new family

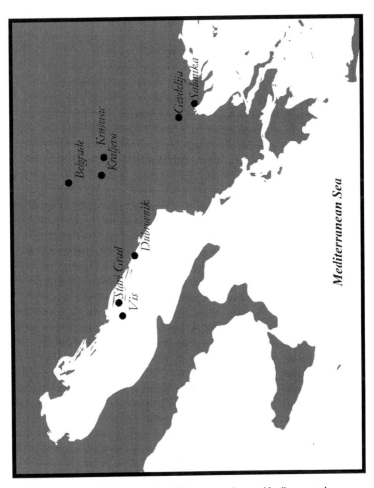

Map 2: The Yugoslav region. This map shows Kraljevo and Kruševac (61km away from each other), south of Belgrade.

From Kraljevo to Melbourne

Part 2

World War II and work at the aircraft factory

In 1934 the King of Yugoslavia sailed to France in a warship to carry out some important diplomatic mission which was unknown to wider circles in Yugoslavia. There were unofficial rumours that an attempt on the King's life was being planned by separatist Croat terrorists with bases in Italy and Hungary. This was known both to the government and to the King and some measures had been taken with the French government.

The cruiser, the Dubrovnik if I am right, with the King on board in admiral's uniform, arrived in the French southern port of Marseilles and was met by the French foreign minister, Barthou. King Alexander got into a car with Barthou next to him and his suite following. French rules provide for three types of escort for the representatives of foreign states. Unfortunately none of these three types of escorts was mounted to meet the King of Yugoslavia, and the only person protecting the King was some colonel (whose name I do not recall) mounted on a horse, who followed the car carrying the King and the French foreign minister, Barthou. The streets through which the King passed held crowds of people that had come to greet the King of Yugoslavia, an ally in the First World War and after it. He met an enthusiatic ovation.

Suddenly a tall man with a large bouquet of flowers came out of the crowd, ran quickly to the car and opened fire from an automatic Mauser – heavy calibre with twenty-five rounds in the magazine! The assassin was immediately attacked by the escorting colonel with his sabre drawn and by the crowd. He was killed before he could be arrested and questioned; the threads of the plot were hidden. The King was fatally wounded by three bullets and the minister, Barthou, killed. The King of Yugoslavia, Alexander, died shortly afterwards in the Yugoslav embassy without regaining consciousness. That was the grievous end of the King's mission to his 'faithful' ally, France. This happened on 9 October, 1934.

The sad news spread like lightning through Yugoslavia. There was weeping everywhere and church services were held for their beloved King. The King's body was taken on board the cruiser Dubrovnik for its last voyage, to Yugoslavia. It is hard to remember and even harder to describe the emotions of the broad masses of the people with which they expressed their love and devotion to their King. Numerous delegations hastened from every corner of the land to pay their last respects to their monarch. Representatives of the Russian emigration marked especially their love and gratitude to the chivalrous King, who had been a father to them and to whom in large measure they owed their prosperity in his hospitable land.

Never in its history had Yugoslavia seen anything like this grand funeral and the emotion felt by the whole country, expressed in tears and grief. Life, however, demands its own and the saying is: The King is dead – long live the King!

At this tragic time for Yugoslavia the heir to the throne, Prince Peter, was ten years old, and his two brothers, Princes Tolislav and Andrew, were even younger. Hence a council of regents was formed of three: Prince Paul, the cousin of the dead King Alexander, and messrs. Perovič and Stankovič. They undertook to manage the affairs of state until Prince Peter attained his majority. Life in Yugoslavia began gradually to return to normal.

As I have said, in January, 1936, I moved to Kraljevo to work at the aircraft factory, where my family and I were caught up in the events preceeding the Second World War. In 1939 war began in Europe as a result of the alliance concluded between Germany and Italy. The two dictators, Hitler and Mussolini, decided that the time had come to put their plans into action, to broaden their influence and expand territorially at the expense of their neighbours.

Hitler's first victim was Austria, where he was born. Austria was 'almost' painlessly annexed to the Third Reich, as the National Socialist Party called Germany. Then the Sudetenland was demanded from Czechoslovakia, which had received it when the state was formed after the First World War. There followed the occupation of Czechoslovakia – almost painlessly. Thereupon Hitler's Minister of Foreign Affairs, Ribbentrop, made moves in Moscow, where an alliance was concluded to divide Poland. Despite heroic resistance, its whole territory was rapidly occupied by German and Soviet troops. The Baltic states were also occupied by Soviet troops to restore the frontier which had existed before the First World War. As we all know, Belgium, Holland, Denmark, Scandinavia and France followed. After an unsuccessful attempt to land in England, Hitler resolved to strike at its colonies in Africa. For this he had to open a route through the Balkans: Yugoslavia and Greece.

There began a diplomatic game between Germany and Yugoslavia. The government of Yugoslavia was inclined to accept Germany's proposal to permit German troops to transit Yugoslav territory on the way to Greece, but this was opposed by the Serbian nationalists, who regarded it as betrayal of their allies in the First World War: France, Britain and Greece. These were supported by certain circles in the church (Bishop Nikolaj of Zica) and the military, particularly the air force (General Simovič).

Consequently there were two camps. The first, mainly Serbs and others who were pro-Yugoslavia, stood for loyalty to their allies in the First World War. The other camp, mainly those who had been part of Austro-Hungary before the First World War, were for an alliance with Germany, believing that it was bound to win and that resistance was pointless. The worst was that this was a relatively small, but well organised and militant section of the Croats, determined on separation from Yugoslavia and the formation of an independent state under the aegis of Germany and with the name of the 'Independent Croatian State'. To the credit of Croatia, its most numerous Horvatska seljačka (people's) partija, which had a majority over the other, militant, party, was against secession and supported the idea of a united Yugoslavia. Unfortunately, Germany was for a break-up of Yugoslavia and fully supported the Croats. When the government concluded a pact with Germany, promising free transit through Yugoslavia to Greece, General Simovič, the commander-in-chief of the air force, supported by the Serb nationalists, demonstrating under the slogan 'Better war than a pact', engineered a coup, placing the seventeen-year-old heir on the throne as King Peter the Second, thus creating the atmosphere and a cause for military conflict with Germany. The German ambassador in Belgrade broke off diplomatic relations, resulting in the air raid on Belgrade on the first day of Easter.

When Germany attacked Yugoslavia, the Croat chauvinists–separatists immediately began a campaign of treachery, sabotage and betrayal. In various areas, particularly in the War Ministry and the administration, where their supporters were in leading positions, the decisions and orders of the top leaders were sabotaged. Thus chaos was caused and the resistance plan disrupted. It was clear to all, of course, that, even if resistance had had full support, it could have lasted longer and caused more bloodshed, and Germany, in all respects stronger than Yugoslavia, would have been victorious.

The German troops advanced in three columns in different directions, dividing Yugoslavia into three, while Dalmatia, Albania and the western part of

Yugoslavia and Greece were occupied by Italian troops, who were strongly resisted by the Greek armies and could not move forward until the whole of Greece was occupied by German troops.

Military operations went on for only twelve days, when a truce was concluded. Leaving a number of their troops to occupy the whole of Yugoslavia, the German units continued their advance into Greece, the last obstacle in the way of their ultimate aim: the leap into Africa!

As I said, I was working on a milling machine at the aircraft factory in Kraljevo for a very good wage. It seemed that I could not wish for a better situation, but the war came, spoilt the game and turned everything upside down! When the war began, retreating army units blew up the big railway bridge 1.5 kilometres from our factory and also part of the factory itself (fortunately all the metal-working machines, lathes, milling machines, special machines and the rest were saved) with the intention that the Germans would not be able to use our factory to continue to produce Dornier aircraft of their own design.

The Yugoslav units retreated hurriedly towards the west – towards the Adriatic Sea – hoping that the British fleet would meet them there, as had been the case in the First World War, but this was not to be. Some units were taken prisoner, and some individuals came home to Kraljevo. The destroyed railway bridge was no hindrance for the German units; they quickly set up a pontoon bridge and their units entered Kraljevo.

The German units who entered Kraljevo behaved very well and there were no incidents. Those inhabitants who had gone away to the villages before the Germans arrived began to drift back to the town. I also went to fetch my family, which was 3 kilometres away in the nearest village with relatives. The German guards readily gave me permission to cross their pontoon bridge.

Life gradually returned to normal and it was soon announced that factory workers should report to the factories (there were two; our aircraft factory and one where railway rolling stock was built) to reactivate them. At our factory, where before the war there had been about 1,000 workers, some 200 came. Some had gone home to various towns, many of them to the newly formed State of Croatia and to Slovenia. The first step was to clear up damage from exploding mines, then restore the various installations and machines. At the same time we fulfilled some orders for the German units in the town. This went on until war began in our homeland, when many of the German formations in Serbia went off to the eastern front. (I have changed the name of Yugoslavia to Serbia, since, after the secession of Croatia, there remained only Serbia in the old borders of 1914.) To maintain order, the German command permitted the Serbian General Nedič to form a government and a properly armed Serbian Guard.

When the Yugoslav army capitulated, far from all its units surrended their arms. For example, Colonel Draža Mihailovič (later promoted by order of King Peter to General), with his staff, formed a substantial detachment and retreated to the mountains, refusing to surrender to the enemy. Other detachments like his were formed to fight the occupiers and the partisan war began. The partisans, although this was not at first evident, were of two kinds: some were Yugoslav nationalists fighting for the kingdom of Yugoslavia, others had communist leanings and looked to the establishment of communism in Yugoslavia.

Shortly after war began in our homeland, partisan units began to concentrate around Kraljevo and to engage in various forms of sabotage: damaging telephone and telegraph lines, railways and roads, bridges etc. These actions evoked a strong reaction on the part of the occupying powers; clashes occurred and there were dead and wounded on both sides. There soon followed an order from German headquarters that 100 local inhabitants would be shot for every German soldier killed. Warning posters appeared everywhere. Because of these activities, the local civil authorities were ordered to guard various sites and communication lines in the vicinity of the town. The local authorities compiled rosters, arranging pairs (unarmed, of course) and indicating the night and the district in which they were to do duty. The result of this measure was nil.

Massacre at Kraljevo

In the beginning all workers worked during the day and went home to their families at the end of the working day. Once, however, during the working day, all the workers were paraded in the factory yard, for some to be called out and separated according to some list. It later became clear that those who were called out were citizens of secessionist Croatia. They were told that in future they would be able to go home after work; the rest after work would spend the night at the factory.

We were given a large cellar to sleep in. For the night two sentries were posted at the door with light machine-guns and with an order to let no one out of the cellar, even for normal needs (two containers were put in for that purpose). We later found out that us workers in the cellar were regarded as hostages.

During the night we would often hear rifle and machine-gun fire and even exploding grenades or mortar bombs. These were the partisans attempting to sieze the town, and the factories in particular, so as to prevent the Germans from putting them into production. This situation did not last long. Early one morning those of us who were in the cellar were mustered in the yard and taken by an indirect route to the railway rolling-stock factory, where we were put into an unfinished building intended for a future locomotive building shop.

There on a grassed area we found a large group of workers from this factory and also residents of Kraljevo and its neighbourhood. All these people were hostages. It was relatively warm in the building, since it was summer, but cold at night. Residents of Kraljevo whose family members had been taken as hostages were ordered to bring blankets and food for their relatives. Hence there were crowds standing all day at the factory gate.

People were frequently called out by name, not to reappear, though sometimes a reason was given for their being called out.

Two days passed and on the third after dinner I was called out and ordered to go home and report to the factory next morning to be at the disposal of the newly appointed chief engineer, who turned out to be our son's godfather. It later became clear that a milling machine operator was needed for repair work and one of my good friends, a Croat by origin, a turner, had named me and added that I had been sent with others to the hostage camp. So I found myself in relative freedom. In the evening, when I walked through the deserted streets and came to the building where my flat was, the building was closed. Our flat was on the first floor and I had to knock at a window on the ground floor and ask them to open the door for me.

Our joy at meeting again was great, since all the families had already been told that we were hostages. Our situation, though disquieting, became nevertheless less dangerous, though the blockade and the clashes continued. So during the day I would work at the factory, have my meals at home, but again spend the night in the cellar with the others. Then there was a rumour that, because of the increasing number of incidents in which German soldiers were killed, a punishment detachment had arrived in town to begin shooting hostages. The number of hostages grew considerably, as all the houses were searched for men, all of whom, from boys to old men, were taken to the camp. The same thing happened in the neighbouring settlements.

A few days later we who spent our nights in the cellar were paraded early in the morning by police armed with machine-guns and by the same route as before taken towards the camp. We were all surprised that we bypassed the camp, supposing the worst – that we were being taken to be shot.

Not far from the railway station, however we were halted outside a small shed. The shed was opened and we were given spades and picks and taken further, but not far. We were halted for a few seconds in front of

100

the gates of a football field surrounded by a tall fence. When the gates opened, our eyes beheld a horrible scene: the left hand side of the field was piled with corpses. I will not begin to describe the emotions and thoughts which overwhelmed me and, I think, all my friends and acquaintances with me in the column.

One of the German police there came up to the foreman of our column and, after a short conversation, the latter took us to the right hand side of the field, where an area was marked out to dig a mass grave. There were others who had arrived before us who were already working in other parts of the field. Before we started work, a German officer, as we were later to discover, the commander of the punishment detachment, announced through an interpreter that we had to finish our work before five o'clock in the evening. Otherwise he threatened to add us to those for whom we were digging the grave. Under the influence of this threat, intense work began. Conversation was forbidden and there were only brief whispered comments. Before midday there was a five-minute break in which we were allowed to smoke, and a second similar break at twelve o'clock, when we could have a few mouthfuls of water.

Meanwhile the guards had had rations of some kind and most probably spirits, since after the twelve o'clock break, some of them and their commander in particular became vicious. We could hear frequent threats, blows from rifle butts etc. When a pit about 2 metres deep (I don't remember exactly) had been dug, the bodies were brought and placed in the pit at a gradually increasing tempo.

People were already tired and exhausted. In some cases people collapsed and, if they were not able to get up again quickly and if they were noticed by too zealous a guard, there were instances where they were killed. I received a blow with a rifle butt, and once even the commander himself called me over, wagging his finger at me and shouting at me, but a soldier standing by signed to me that I should go away and I ran away from trouble.

My head began to spin and, having dragged a corpse to the pit, I fell into the pit with it.

When I came to, there was one of my friends leaning over to hide me from the guards, but a guard standing close to the pit, my friends told me later, seeing me fall, turned his back on the pit. When I came to, he noticed, smiled and tossed me a cigarette. After this my friends would not let me up out of the pit. So the threat passed and I remained in the pit until the end of this terrible work, helping my friends as much as I could.

We went on with this foul work until dark. When the guard commander who had brought us mustered us to take us back to the aircraft factory, where we spent our nights under guard, the commander of the punishment detachment demanded that we be handed over to him to be added to the number of hostages to be shot. We were saved by the guard commander, who refused to hand us over, saying that we had been given to him to carry out tasks for the army of occupation and that he would not give us up without an order from the military command. So, late in the evening, we returned to the factory, where a big supper with chunks of pork awaited us. Many of us however, including me, had lost our appetite after what we had been through!

The next day my friends were again taken off to the same work, and on the third day also, but on these two days, they said, there was no longer the terror of the first day. On the second and third day I and a few friends were sent to work at the factory, making parts for the army's various needs.

Our situation did not improve and the threat remained. Our Russian colony representatives managed to save some among the hostages from execution; nevertheless, of about 250 Russians, 46 were shot. When representatives of our colony pointed out to the German command that we were former soldiers who had fought against communism, they replied, 'Why then, since you know all the local inhabitants, have you not pointed out a single communist in your town?' Subsequently they gave this advice: join the Russian Corps or go to Germany as tradesmen to work in your own specialisation. To discuss this question, I arranged a family conference with my wife and mother-in-law to decide what to do. Our child was nearly two. I had no wish to go to Germany and abandon my family, since this would mean a long separation. To go off to the rebels was not only a threat to my family, but also against my convictions as a White soldier. There remained one course only: the Russian Corps.

The only option

Registration began, then a medical examination, and all those of us who were passed fit began to prepare to leave, settling all our personal and family affairs. Having got rid of everything I could, selling for very little everything not needed for my wife's move to her sister in another town and saying good-bye to them, in December, 1941, I left for the city of Belgrade (the capital of Yugoslavia), where the Russian Corps was being formed.

Without any special formalities, since I was still relatively young and fit (at 39) in comparision with many, when one would often come across men of 50, 60 and even 70, I was accepted and sent to Corps headquarters, to which the 2nd Regiment, already formed, was going. The completed regiments were being sent to various areas to guard various sites, such as: lines of communication, mines and other sites of military importance.

Many of us were disappointed to find that our main objective, to continue the fight under the Russian Tricolour for the liberation of our homeland from communism, was left hanging in the air. Nevertheless we had hopes that the time would come!

Soon after my arrival and the departure of the 2nd Regiment, there arrived from the town of Novi Sad an already partly formed battalion, the Novosadsky, under the command of a general of the White Army, Major General of Artillery Cherepov. I was posted to 1st Company, to Colonel Treskin, who had served in the First World War in the Life Guards Volynsky Regiment (what a coincidence: my grandfather did his regular service and served in the Turkish War of 1877/78 in that regiment!); my platoon commander was Colonel Lyubomirov and section commander Captain Mikhaylov.

This strange situation of officers taking such minor posts was nothing new, since at one time, 1918-21, in the White Army there were officers' regiments and officers often served as privates. Both Colonel Treskin and Colonel Lyubomirov were genuine officers of the old Imperial Army with its traditions and were very sympathetic in dealing with those under them ie. their subordinates. One could not say the same of Captain Mikhaylov, who often drank heavily and when inebriated terrorised his subordinates. Consequently there were constant complaints about him and he was dismissed from the Corps. Just at that time there arrived from Novi Sad my former regimental commander in the Crimea (as a colonel), Lieutenant-General Apukhtin (who had served in the Imperial Army in Her Majesty's Life Guards Ulan Regiment). Hearing my name, he came up to me and recalled our stay in Gallipoli, the training detachment, promotion, our choir (in which I sang), which he would often invite into his tent for everyone's entertainment. The 2nd Platoon turned out to be commanded by my former squadron commander in the Crimea, Colonel Rubets of Her Majesty's Life Guards Cuirassier Regiment, who also recognised me when we met. As the battalion was being formed, we had drill and lecture sessions, since we were being familiarised with German Army regulations and drill, which differed greatly from the old Russian drill (although I had not gone through Russian infantry drill, since I had served in the cavalry).

Active duty

Finally the day came for our battalion to leave for the area of the 1st Regiment, to the small settlement of Zajača, where there was a mine which we were to guard against the partisans in the area.

On the hills round the mine there were dug-outs in which guard detachments of 5-6 men observed the country around day and night, setting sentries. The nights were uncomfortable, particularly when we heard wolves howling, but duty is duty and we had to accept the situation and await better days! We were armed with rifles and every guard post was issued with an ancient (First World War vintage) Chauchat machine-gun. I was not pleased to be rewarded with such a machine-gun. It was a miracle of French production with a vicious kick, noisy, and prone to jamming.

I had learnt to use a machine-gun when I was in the White Army, but these were British and German makes, much better than it. I had only two spells in that dug-out. Chance rescued me! Easter was approaching and a number of men from each company were given leave. Since there were few in our company who wished to go, I was one of the lucky ones. As if on wings I set off on the long journey! I first had to use a cart to get to regimental headquarters, then a lorry to Belgrade, to the corps headquarters, where I obtained travel documents to the town of Kruševac where my family was. From Belgrade I made my way by rail home to Kruševac. Certainly there were few trains, mostly at night and always overcrowded. Though one was often standing, it was warm and it was fast. It had been four months since I had left for the corps and this was an unexpected surprise for my wife and 2 ½-year-old son ! I will not try to describe our meeting: everyone will understand without a description! Two weeks passed like a single day and I had to get ready to set off again!

Before I left we went to a photographer to have a souvenir of this meeting. We still have the photograph.

On the return journey, when I called at corps headquarters, I was told that our battalion had been transferred to another district on the river Drina and, while waiting for transport, I was held up for a few days in Belgrade. Then transport turned up and I made it to my company. Guard duty began again. In this district there were also units of the Serbian Guard with the same orders as our company. We were stationed close to the river Drina (a fairly wide, fast river) and, together with the Serbian Guard, we often rescued refugees from the other bank of the river escaping bloody massacres by the Croats, who, extreme chauvinists and Catholics, were persecuting the Orthodox Serbs. Sometimes it came to exchanges of fire between us and the Croat gangs. Otherwise the time passed fairly quietly, since there were no communist partisans in the vicinity.

As I have described, our battalion was the first to be formed. Meanwhile, two more battalions of our regiment were being formed in Belgrade. When the last two battalions were ready, they were sent to the south of Serbia, to the region called Macedonia, with its chief town of Skopje, where regimental headquarters were situated. Our battalion was ordered to march to the town of Užice to entrain for Skopje and then to our post in the town of Vučitern. This town and its vicinity are populated mainly by Albanians, Muslims with mosques, and reminded us of Turkey.

Some days later I was summoned to battalion headquarters, where I was ordered to collect my things and the documents necessary and proceed to Corps headquarters in Belgrade. When I asked what happened, I was told that I was being put under the orders of the director of the Corps headquarters armoury because of my knowledge of weapons. I was very pleased with this transfer, since I would be able to spend a few days with my family on the way. Moreover, serving in Belgrade, I would have more opportunity to visit my family. My arrival in Kruševac was a big, unexpected surprise for my family. It was an even bigger surprise that now I would be able to visit them more often.

After spending a week with my family, I set off as directed to Belgrade. I was already expected at the armoury in Belgrade. Let me go back a little; while I was in the Corps, from joining it and until I was sent to Zajača, I would often meet a friend from Kruševac who worked in the same building in the military factory at Kraljevo. During these meetings he introduced me to his superior (a former cavalry captain). They advised me to transfer to their workshop. I agreed and they began to try to arrange a transfer, but there were some hold-ups. This friend of mine, Nikolay Lakayev, who worked in the armoury as a tradesman and had known me earlier, helped to obtain the transfer, for which I was very grateful.

So there began for me a new environment, better working conditions and, most important, the opportunity to see my family more often. In time I would set off every second Saturday in the evening for the railway station and travel home on the night train. In the middle of the night, when no one dared to be out on the streets, I could walk home because I wore military uniform and was armed. At the station in Belgrade I used to see civilians, old men and women, some of them having been discharged from hospital and still not fully recovered, who could not find a seat in a carriage (the carriages were all packed), while often young people who had found a seat did not consider it their duty to give up their seat to the weak, the old and sometimes the sick.

Once when I was standing in the crowd waiting for the soldiers guarding the exit to the platform to open the gate, I caught sight of a middle-aged woman carrying a small boy of about 9 or 10. When the gate opened and the crowd rushed it, she was pushed aside and tried vainly to get through. I pushed through to her and asked what was the matter with the boy. She replied that he could not walk, because his leg was broken and in plaster. I suggested that she give me the boy and keep close behind me.

Using my privilege as a soldier, I quickly overcame all obstacles and reached the carriages with my burden: the woman also managed to follow me. There were a lot of passengers at every carriage and, having no choice, we went up to the nearest carriage and climbed in. All the seats were taken and there were many people standing, glad that, even standing, they would get to their destination.

Not finding a seat (I had to find somewhere for the sick boy, since I could not hold him for long and he could not stand on one leg), in the end I spotted a young man and asked him to give up his seat to the boy, which he did. His neighbour jumped up and offered me his seat; I thanked him for his kind offer and remained standing, emphasing that my main aim had been to find a seat for the sick boy.

When we got to the station where I had to change trains, I wished the boy and his mother a good journey onward and left the carriage. Once on the platform, I felt someone behind me pull me by the arm and try to give me something. When I looked round, it was the boy's mother looking at me with her eyes full of tears and asking me to take a little gift as a sign of gratitude: it was some money. This touched me to tears, but I would not take the money, explaining that I was myself a father with a wife and son and was going to visit them. So we parted. Many times, arriving home at night, I would help home those who, since they were civilians, did not have the right to walk the streets at night. In this way I tried to some extent to repay my debt to the hospitable Serbian people, now in such a grave situation, but which once, in 1921, had welcomed me (with the White Army units) and given us all refuge, rescuing us from a grave (morally and materially) situation.

So my and my family's life passed without significant changes. At work I gradually improved and established my position in the workshop, taking courses which gave me the right to promotion.

When a year had passed, I managed to get into a course for arms and equipment officers. When I completed the course, I was promoted to NCO and made arms and equipment officer in my company and at the same time second-in-command of the machine-gun platoon, since, working in the armoury, I had studied all the types of weapons used by the Corps. In this new position I had to introduce a new inventory method for weapons, ammunition and all kinds of equipment also. When, within a few months, this was done, I was recommended for and awarded a Second Class Cross for my work.

Days, weeks and months passed. It was nearly the second half of 1944. The front was approaching from the east and the possibility of withdrawal from Belgrade was being discussed. The evacuation began of various rear institutions and of civilians wishing to leave the zone close to the front in good time. On one of my visits to the family, I persuaded my wife to get ready for a possible rapid evacuation and to be ready to move at any moment. Meanwhile my wife's relatives were trying to persuade her to remain at home. Fearing that my wife could remain there under the influence of her mother and her relatives, I asked my commanding officer for two days leave to bring my family to Belgrade for evacuation. Although no leave was permitted, my commanding officer took the responsibility of agreeing to give me two days' leave to evacuate my wife and son. When I arrived home, I managed to persuade them of the necessity of evacuation, be it only for a short time. So I brought them to Belgrade, to the Russian House, where all the formalities needed for the coming evacuation were completed. When they had spent two days in the Russian House, I accompanied my wife and 5-year-old son with a convoy of Corps families to the railway station of Zemun on the other bank of the Danube. (The bridge across the Danube had been blown up in 1941 and trains could not cross it; it was crossed only by road transport.) At Zemun I settled my wife and son in a carriage and we parted: this was in September 1944. We met again after the war ended in December 1945. The war had ended on 9 May, 1945, but the search took a little more than seven months and the separation a little more than fifteen months. I found my family in one of the refugee camps in Bavaria (70 kilometres south of Munich). Our meeting was very joyful and touching and it is difficult for me to describe.

But now I must return to my story.

Having seen my family off on their way to Germany, I returned to Belgrade, where preparations were already being made for evacuation. As I said above, I had been made second-in command of the machine-gun platoon under Major-General Nazimov, formerly of the White Army, a very nice, modest and responsive officer.

Shortly before the evacuation of Belgrade, General Nazimov fell ill and was sent to hospital; I was not to meet him again. When General Nazimov left, I had reluctantly to take command of the platoon – temporarily, I was promised by the company commander, since I had a great deal of my own responsibilities with regard to arming and equipping the company. Taking command of the machine-gun platoon (there were three Maxim guns with a good supply of ammunition and spare parts), I handed over some of my responsibilities as arms and equipment officer to my second-in-command and began to prepare for evacuation. I was in charge of three horse-drawn carts and a platoon of forty. All the platoon's equipment had been loaded on the carts, so we were ready to move at any time.

At last we got the order to proceed to the station of Topčider, where we were to entrain. We then set off into the unknown, since none of us knew where we were being sent. In the evening our train stopped at the station of Lapovo, from which one line went to Kruševac and the other to Niš. We soon set off for Kruševac, so I had an opportunity to visit my wife's family ie. her mother, brother-in-law, sister and children, since we stopped there two hours. This was the last meeting in our life. Thereafter we could only write to them, as after the war we lived in Bavaria for four years, and emigrated in 1949 to Australia, where we are now (1983).

Going on from Kruševac, we reached Čačak, where we got out and were posted on the outskirts of the town to guard the approaches to it from various directions. Our company took guard of two roads, one to Arilje, the other to Požegu Užice (the roads forked there). My platoon with three Maxim machine-guns was stationed on the left, and Colonel Podolsky's platoon with two French light machine-guns on the right. On the road to Arilje there was a 24-hour guard with two Maxims, each with two machine-gunners, and another 24-hour guard with one Maxim on the embankment closer to the town. The road to Požegu was also guarded round the clock by two light machine-guns. A few days later we had attached to us men from the Požarevačka brigada (Dražinovci), who also took part in guarding the roads. I managed to get to know some of the men in this brigade, young students who for some reason were friendly and trusting with me. They advised me to be careful, because, they said, the brigade was a mixed lot!

There were rumours that the Požarevačka brigada was preparing to retreat into Montenegro to await on the Adriatic shore a British ship which would take them on board for transport to some other sector. Towards evening a big group entered our district, evidently the officers in command of the brigade, headed by its colonel. When I went up to them and said that I was in command of this unit, they began to persuade me to join them. When I replied that they should approach my battalion commander, since I could do so only on his orders, they left. Their proposal made me think that they might try some trick to make us join them, because they greatly outnumbered us. Thereupon I went to the 1st Platoon commander (Colonel of the

Russian Service S.N. Podolsky) and shared my suspicions.

My suspicions seemed strange to him, since he believed that relations between us and the Dražinovci[17] were good and that there was no reason to be suspicious. Since I insisted, he asked me what I wanted. I said: 'I want you, since you are the senior officer and you have a telephone, to get permission from the company or even battalion commander that tonight, since the Požarevačka brigada is leaving, we should not put out the machine guns, but leave them in the guard-house, and also withdraw the sentries after twelve o'clock and post them at the guard-house!'

'Do you really think that the Dražinovci could cause some unpleasantness? After all we have very good relations with them', he replied.

I answered 'there is a war on and anything can happen and God helps those who help themselves.'

I stand by my opinion. Sergey Nikolayevich went off and returned some minutes later to say that he had rung the battalion commander, who had told him to act at his discretion, to which I replied that I stand by my proposal.

Thereupon I mustered all the men of my platoon, described the situation, and ordered them to be ready that night to open fire at any moment, giving each of them a post. Each of us had a rifle and two hand-grenades, so we could put up a good resistance. Our machine-guns were adapted for steel belts, were free of warping and other jams and had plenty of ammunition.

---

[17] Serb nationalist and monarchist paramilitary fighters loyal to General Dragoljub "Draža" Mihailović (commonly known as Chetniks).

In the evening two Dražinovci officers and their wives, who were accommodated in one of the rooms of the building, said good-bye to us and left. Several days before this I had noticed one of the officers of the Požarevačka brigada coming out of our building as I approached, which made me suspicious. So I asked my men why that officer had been in our building. They said that he had been very interested in the working of the machine-guns and had asked to be shown how to use them.

Next day I went out of the building and kept watch from the next yard. When the same officer went in, I waited a little, then followed him in and found him examining our machine-guns and interrogating my men. The officer, caught napping, was most embarrassed and did not know how he should behave. I asked him why it was that he had entered my guard-house without asking me, since, as an officer, he knew quite well the rule which forbade that, particularly as we were in position. So I ordered him to leave immediately and in future not to set foot in our positions. With this he left and I did not see him again. But that incident also gave me grounds for suspicion that some in that brigade were ill-intentioned.

It was evening, but the sun had not yet set. Suddenly, from the direction of the forest, there appeared a group of soldiers. When they came closer, it was clear that they were officers in Yugoslav uniform, three senior officers of the Požarevačka brigada. We exchanged greetings and a conversation began, in which it turned out that their lieutenant-colonel in command was proposing that I and my men should join them and go to Montenegro, where there were British ships waiting to take them to some other sector.

To this proposal I replied to him that I could not do this without orders and that he should apply to my battalion commander. If he ordered me to, then I would obey the order. He made no reply to this, since as later became clear, he had already another plan – which would fail – because I also had my plan, which fortunately succeeded.

The lieutenant-colonel and his suite left and night soon fell. In the evening movement had begun from the vicinity of Čačka towards Požegu Užice. There were carts and men on foot moving; the movement went on for a long time and ceased as morning approached. By evening, shortly before midnight, our sentries had been withdrawn from the machine-gun nests and the whole platoon was mustered in the guard-house.

Suddenly from outside I heard the voice of Sergey Nikolayevich Podolsky calling me by name and patronymic. When I asked what had happened, he replied that the Yugoslav officers wished to say good-bye to me. I took my Browning out of its holster and began to go down stairs quietly. When I approached the gate, I heard words spoken in Serbian: 'You are under arrest'. I turned quickly, ran up the stairs into the guard-house, roused everybody and ordered them to prepare for defensive action.

Again a voice was heard outside: 'Surrender. You are surrounded'.

'We will not surrender; if you wish, take us by force!', I said.

The reply came, 'But you will all die'.

'Maybe, but you will be the first and maybe us afterwards', I replied and at that moment I noticed some people running round outside.

'Halt, or I open fire!', I shouted loudly.

There was a shout in reply: 'Please do not open fire'.

I replied, 'Then go away!'.

A few minutes passed and then the movement outside ceased. The minutes went by and it began to get light as morning approached. From the direction of the 1st Platoon we heard voices asking what had happened to us. When they learnt that everything was in order with us, they told us that, since the Dražinovci had tricked their commander into going with them, they had formed a command group of three, Colonel Nazarov, Prince Maksumov and Lieutenant Ivanov. Otherwise everything was in order.

When it was fully light, a messenger came from company headquarters to our neighbours, the 1st Platoon, to find out what had happened to us. Company headquarters was very worried, since the Dražinovci had taken away the whole of the 1st Company together with one officer. There was only the commander left, who by chance had been absent at the time. Half the 2nd Company had also been taken away: the company commander and the other half of the company had been at another location which the Dražinovci had not been able to reach.

As morning came, a cart arrived with tea and provisions. Before we had finished breakfast, firing began from the direction of the forest. This was evidently the brigade commander, angry at the outcome of the attempt to take our guard unit away by force of arms (machine-guns, to be more accurate), trying to pay us back for his failure. The firing continued. I have omitted one detail. In the early morning, before the cart with tea arrived, S.M. Podolsky, the commander of the

1st Platoon, returned. The Draživovci had released him, since their objective had been to take us all, and, above all the machine-guns. Since their plan had failed, they had no need for the platoon commander alone. That would have been extra trouble for them.

So the exchange of fire continued. We placed our machine-guns back in position. The telephone, which had been out of action (the Draživovci had cut the wire), was repaired and communication with headquarters restored.

Fearing that the Draživovci would use their superiority in numbers to try to attack our position, we were sent reinforcements under the command of Oberleutnant Dubrov, which took them in the flank, and they withdrew further into the forest. During the exchange of fire, one soldier in my platoon was wounded in the leg, but the wound was a light one and he remained at his post.

When he had completed his action, Oberleutnant Dubrov brought his group to our post, where we inspected our machine-gun nests, the firing having then died down. Just then my second-in-command, NCO (Second-Lieutenant) Tikhomirov, was wounded in the shoulder by a stray bullet from the direction of the forest. He was taken first to the hospital and then on to Germany. I did not meet him again, but I had news that he had recovered and was living somewhere in Germany.

The war's end and reunion

The war ended. As the Red Army approached, evacuation of the family to Austria and further, the difficult path of the Russian Corps, from Belgrade, across Serbia, Bosnia, Croatia, Slovenia to Klagenfurt, surrender of arms to the British[18]. Fate of wife and son unknown for fourteen months, and the search for them. Finally reunion with the family in Bavaria. Four years of life as refugees and finally departure for Australia. On arrival in Australia my wife and I found work and our son went to school. Solving the problem of existence we join the Russian Orthodox Community abroad in which with other parishioners collect funds for our own church which we soon acquired. In 1954 I was elected churchwarden in the parish and, together with many other parishioners began a restoration of the empty church building, which had been neglected for many years, to adapt it for Orthodox services.

Russian House in Australia

After four years of hard and arduous work in the parish, when normal church life had been restored, I withdrew from parish work to work for the Russian National Government, where I raised the question of the organisation of a Russian House in which it would be possible to unite the cultural and national section of Russians. People were found who were willing to support this idea and there soon came into being a new organisation: the Russian House in Melbourne. After three years of arduous and devoted work a large two-storey building was bought (in extremely run-down condition). A huge refurbishment was carried out, and, at the present time, the Russian House lives a full

---

[18] The surrender to the British took place on 12th of May 1945.

cultural life. Apart from the older generation, it is a meeting place also for young people, who will take our place and who take part in the management and the work of the Russian House alongside the older generation. It was hard for us to leave Russian Melbourne, having lived there thirty-two years, but we have the consolation that here in Canberra there is a strong Russian colony developing quite quickly around the newly built church. Given skillful leadership, there is a possibility of progress. The years pass and

[The manuscript ends here abruptly]

EFIMIJ MOKRIJ

Some notes

(on a loose page, written in the 3rd person)

Thirty years ago, in July 1932 in the Uspensky church in the town of Kruševac (Yugoslavia), Yevfimy Vasilyevich Mokry and Slava Melentjevna Milovanovič were married. The witnesses were: for the bridegroom Colonel of the Russian Service Aleksandr Ivanovich Degtyarev and for the bride Colonel of the Yugoslav Army Stanko Turudija. Having lived for about five years there, they, on account of the poor health of SM, moved on medical advice to Kraljevo, where SM had been born. In 1939 they had a son, Alexander, at present fit and living with his family in Canberra. EV found a good position in Kraljevo at the aircraft factory and they began to live a quiet, peaceful and happy life – but not for long. The Second World War broke out and would reach Kraljevo. In 1941 Yugoslavia was occupied by the German army. The aircraft factory was partly destroyed and closed. There were two options: 1) go to Germany to work (the factory at Kraljevo made aircraft of a German type) or 2) join the partisans. The third option was to volunteer for the Russian Corps, which was beginning to be formed. EV took the latter course, intending to go on serving Russia as he had begun in the White Army.

Russian House

The family in Melbourne.

INTERNATIONAL REFUGEE ORGANIZATION
(I. R. O.)
DISPLACED PERSONS PROFESSIONAL
TESTING BOARD

J. 5

B. 6243 grossnaschau

CERTIFICATE No. 10209

This is to certify that bearer of the certificate

Mr. MOKRIJ Efimij

was given theoretical and practical tests by IRO Professional Testing
Board. The above named has been qualified as a *Machine*

milling operator;

with 12 years of experience in this profession.

President of the
Testing Board IRO
Univ. Prof. J. Zviseher

JRO

Leader of Testing Commission
for

Area Employment Officer

IRO Team 1066

Munich, 6. II. 1948

Refugee papers: Educational
qualifications, machine milling operator:
February 1948.

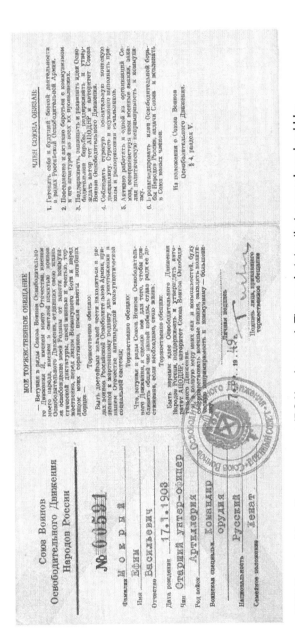

1949 Russian Liberation movement (POA) union card. The card states that a member should be ready at any time to take up arms against Bolshevism, when summoned. The information on the left states Efimij's rank: artillery gun commander.

A

Appendices

Appendices

A: Love letter from Efimij to Slava, 1932[19]

My dearest sweetheart!

When I tell you that all my thoughts and feelings are about you, there is no place for doubt because I am telling you the truth. Every single moment I can steal away from my everyday obligations is dedicated to you – I use it either to write to you or to finish some affairs that might influence our future life together. As you can see, even though I've already sent you a letter this morning (and I still have not received a letter from you since you left Kragujevac), after I had finished my lunch I had one more hour before work so I am writing to you again, to tell you about my feelings and thoughts in the letter, since I cannot do it otherwise. I hope to receive your letter this afternoon, and I will finish this one in the evening.

If only you knew how eager I am to get your letter – to see if you arrived home safely and how you are feeling now, how your Mum welcomed you and whether you are thinking about me. One hour of

---

[19] Translated from Serbian.

waiting and anticipation is like one day for me now, and one day – it is a whole year. I cannot wait for Easter – to be able to put my arms around you and kiss your sweet little mouth, and do those other things,….you know, which you did not allow me to do at first but then you let me – do you remember? I am overwhelmed with unusual joy when I think about those happy moments I spent with you, that day and that last night! I cannot wait for the day when I'll have you by my side again, when I will listen to you talking and feel your sweet gentle kisses.

I am just as eager when I work on preparing for our future life together, constantly thinking how I could please you more, how I could make our life better. But, it is impossible to foresee everything, believe me and I hope that you won't hold it against me if something is not done according to your wishes, because we must take into account not only our taste but also common sense and price – you know well that I will bear most of the expenses and as I am not a wealthy man I must take the utmost care about how much will be spent and what for. We must not get into debt because the consequences would be very bad; therefore, I intend to leave some money aside for our future, so that we would not have to start our life together flat broke.

We must think about the future and, if God will have it, my son and daughter (if it is your wish to have them with me – and I support your wish completely). Furthermore, I've already thought about the apartment, so I applied for the one in the *Colony*[20]. I asked for a small 2-room apartment, detached if possible. In a few

---

[20] 'Colony' is actually a part of Kragujevac that's called *Kolonija* in Serbian. It was built in the period 1927-1929, so I guess that's what he meant (*Trans Note*).

days, and maybe after Easter, I will do my best to hasten the issue of getting the apartment, with the help of a friend, but if I don't get it by the beginning of June by some chance, I will personally ask the Colony supervisor for the permission to move in with someone who has a few extra spare rooms, temporarily, of course, until I get my own apartment. As for the furniture, I asked around a bit and it is general advice not to buy too much furniture and spend too much money on that matter; anyway, we'll see about that later and we'll find the solution somehow. The most important thing for me is that you are satisfied. A propos the wedding, try to talk your Mum into letting us get married in Gruza, because, as you already know, it would be much more expensive to get married in Kraljevo, especially for Mum, and it would not be easy for her to suffer the consequences of those unnecessary expenses. That is what Mr Milenko and Mr Pavle think and I agree with them completely; so, when we all meet in Kraljevo for Easter then we will decide on all the matters and make Mum give us consent to get married in Gruza.

Concerning the gifts which I should bring for Easter, I want to tell you that I will not take anything from Kragujevac; could you please talk to Mum about that – you two decide together on what you would like to have, pick the presents in the stores and they could keep them until I arrive. I will pay for the presents when I get there and everything will be fine. I want you to decide and choose the presents on time because we won't have much time on our hands to look for them, and it might also happen that you both lose your nerves and then, naturally, you'll pick the things offhand which are neither to your taste nor practical.

Now I am back again from my afternoon work and unfortunately I see that I still haven't received your letter. I am terribly sorry but nevertheless I don't blame you and I am not angry with you because I know that you are very busy now that Vrbica1 and Easter holidays are approaching. But I have to ask you not to be angry with me when I neglect our correspondence a bit, and that will be around 25th – 27th April. Those days are extremely busy for me every month because I have to manage the bills of exchange that are due and collect monthly payments from those who pay off their debts on a monthly basis. So, this month and the next one, from 25th to 27th, I will have quite a lot of work to do because I must try to collect as much money as possible for the things we will need and for our wedding. You yourself know very well that our future life together depends on this; therefore I give my utmost attention to collecting money. I hope that I will arrange everything just fine, with the help of God.

I still don't know what expenses you and your Mum are expecting – you should let me know so that I can act accordingly and bring enough money when I come over there for Easter. One more thing, I forgot that we must buy wedding rings in Kraljevo when I arrive; at least that is what we agreed upon while you were here.

We must definitely avoid unnecessary costs because we will need many things and also there will be costs which we don't foresee yet – we will not have too much money and to get into debt in these critical times would be too dangerous. And it would not be a good idea to spend every dime even if we had some extra money.

So, my sweetheart, if you don't receive my letters regularly don't get angry and upset, but instead bear in mind that my thoughts and feelings are with you, always, and the only reason for not writing to you is that I am too busy, which will happen on 25th-27th April. I believe that I will write my last letter to you on Wednesday, 27th, and on Friday, at 5.10 AM, as it seems, I will be on my way to Kraljevo to hold my baby, my darling sweetheart!...

As for your letters, write to me if you can, a few words at least, so that I know and have some kind of proof that you are thinking about me. If I receive 2 letters from you by Easter, I will be pleased and satisfied. My darling, don't work too hard, you are so delicate, it might do you harm, take care of your health both for your and for my sake. Work must be done, but we must take care of our health, it is more important than anything else. I think I won't be able to write to you tomorrow even if I get your letter, but I will definitely write to you the day after tomorrow so that you can enjoy reading my letters that you fell in love with; but, when I come over there for Easter, then you must fall in love with me, otherwise I will be jealous of my letters and will make them repulsive in the future. While I am not by your side you can be in love with the letters, but when I am with you, forget about the letters and be in love with me. How is Mum's health? Give her my warmest regards. Also, give my regards to everyone I know in your neighbourhood. And kindest regards to you and your Mum from Mr Pavle, Mrs Zenja and Sura.

My dearest sweetheart, be well and think about me.

Countless kisses,
your Efimij
(Kragujevac, 20th April 1932)

Grafenaschau camp.

B: Alexander's memories of his father[21]

The region where my father was born, on 30 January, 1903, was flat, but undulating country with extremely rich soil. It is part of the black earth region of the country. The scenery is pleasant, although there are no mountains. The Mokrij family were quite prosperous farmers. I think they owned some 100 acres of land when my father was growing up. During the collectivization in the 1930s, they were classified as Kulaks[22] and the land was expropriated and my grandfather expelled to somewhere in Siberia, I think.

*

Whilst he served in the White Army, in Czar Nicholas II's mother's regiment, and therefore was a Cuirassier of Her Highness Maria Fyodorovna, my father was the member of a reconnaissance unit. Maria Fyodorovna used to send Christmas cards to all the former members of her regiment until her death in 1927[23]. I don't know to what extent he participated in the various battles which occurred between the White Army and the Bolshevik forces, but apparently he fell ill with typhoid fever just before a famous battle in the South of Russia, in which the cavalry of the famous Bolshevik cavalry commander and subsequent Marshall, Budenny, took part and inflicted a heavy defeat on the White Army. Falling ill when he did may well have saved my father's life.

---

[21] Alexander Mokrij wrote a family history from which this is taken.

[22] A derisive term for those Russian farmers who were rich at the time of the 1917 Revolution.

[23] Actually 13 October 1928.

My father told me how he, for what I think was a period of several months, travelled in railway carriages in his condition and apparently only recovered when he disembarked with the White Army in the Crimea…

*

The ships on which the remnants of the White Army travelled [from the Crimea across the Black Sea] were overcrowded to the point of bursting, but some civilians managed to take with them all kinds of valuables and take up more space than was necessary. I also remember my father mentioning that during the trip he was able to collect some Madeira wine from a leaking container on the ship.

The fleet sailed past Istanbul and most of the remnants of the White Army - I think some 75,000 officers and men disembarked at Gallipoli. Cossack units, however, disembarked at the island of Lemnos. My father described Gallipoli as being a rocky, rather barren, place and the harbour there as full of sunken allied ships with their masts sticking above the water. Only recently, I discovered how accurate this description was and how heavy the Allied losses were there. My father could not have dreamt that nearly thirty years later he would migrate to a country which considered that its national identity was intimately connected with Gallipoli and that this place contained ground which was hallowed as far as this nation was concerned.

*

The units of the White Army at Gallipoli led a very Spartan existence and experienced considerable privations. I think that my father spent up to six months there, but at the end of this period was able to

135

migrate to Yugoslavia, which accepted him. Of all the Russians who left their country between 1917 and 1923 because of the October Revolution, the Russian Civil War, and their aftermath - altogether more than one million persons - 30,000 settled in Yugoslavia. The remainder migrated to China, the USA, Poland, Germany, France, Great Britain, Spain, Holland, Denmark, Belgium, Switzerland, Italy, Austria, Czechoslovakia, Hungary, Sweden, Finland, Estonia, Latvia, Lithuania, Rumania, Bulgaria, Greece, Turkey, Brazil, and Ethiopia. The main destinations were China, France, Germany, the USA, and Poland. My impression is that even this list is not exhaustive. I have met Russians who had lived in Persia, or Egypt, for example.

*

Having been born just after the outbreak of the Second World War, my earliest childhood coincided with this war and it was exposed to some of its horrors. When I was one and a half years old, my father was interned in the factory in which he worked, along with the other workers, by the German occupying army as a hostage. One hundred of these people were shot by the German's for each German who was killed by the Partisans (communist-led guerrillas). My father barely escaped this fate. During the process of carrying towards a mass grave the bodies of some of those who were shot he almost fainted and fell, apparently on recognizing a friend among them, whereupon one of the German guards put a gun to my father's head. As he was about to pull the trigger, in accord with the order, that person reacted to their grizzly task like my father did.

A friend of my father's interceded on his behalf and pleaded with the German guard not to shoot him - emphasizing that my father was a good man and that he had an infant son. Fortunately, the German relented and instead of shooting my father ordered him to go into one of the ditches in which those who were shot were being buried and make more room for the bodies. As a result of the above incident, my father's hair turned grey.

I was too young to have any memory of the incident, or what was occurring in the household during my father's internment. One can imagine the grief and suffering which was experienced by my mother and grandmother at the time….

*

While we were trying to keep ahead of the Red Army and reach Germany, father was retreating with other members of the Russian Corp and the German forces from Yugoslavia. During their retreat, they encountered Partisan and Soviet forces in the town of Čačak, not far from Kraljevo. For the first time they encountered the much feared Katyusha multiple rocket launchers, which the Soviets used with such deadly effect.

A friend of my father's took up a dangerous position which my father would otherwise have occupied, because this friend considered that because my father was married and had a child, whilst he was single, this was the right thing to do. For the fourth time in his life, my father barely escaped death, as this friend was killed whilst occupying this position. It would be appropriate for members of the Mokrij family to say prayers for this noble man's soul.

A religious person cannot but help see God's intervention in relation to those occasions in which my father barely escaped losing his life. Unless they turned out as they did, some of them would have resulted in the extinction of that branch of the Mokrij family…

*

The retreat across the whole of Yugoslavia was long and arduous, but I have no information regarding the other events which took place. All I know is that the units in which my father served reached Austria when the Western Allies were already there and that they surrendered to them.

Whilst there, they were visited by members of the Soviet Army, who attempted to persuade them to return to the Soviet Union. They were not handed over to the Soviet troops like units in the Austrian town of Lienz, however, who comprised Cossack units and among whom were many civilians. Some of these people committed suicide by diving off the bridge across the river in that town, rather than fall into the hands of the Soviet army. Some of those who were handed over were not even Soviet citizens and even those who were not should not have been handed over because they had surrendered to the British and international law required that they should be their prisoners.

This was disregarded and the British, with great callousness, handed these people over to the Soviet troops. They also tricked the officers by pretending that they were taking them to attend a conference with the British military authorities.

Many of these people were executed, but we knew one in Melbourne who was not. The latter, who was a Russian who had Yugoslav citizenship, was eventually released from a prisoner-of-war camp and was allowed to migrate to Australia to join his daughter.

One of our friends in Canberra, Andrei Zosko, along with his mother who was Croatian and two brothers and a sister, was among those who were forcibly -repatriated from Lienz. He has mentioned that a priest was shot by the troops during a disturbance which accompanied the forcible repatriation. They were sent to a camp in Siberia.

His father was a member of a Cossack detachment and he was also repatriated. He is convinced that his father was shot. Andrei was 14 at the time of the repatriation and I think he spent one year or so at the camp. He claims that they were quite well treated and expressed considerable surprise that this occurred. The family managed to escape from the camp and made their way to Moscow. On reaching there, they claimed that they were Yugoslav citizens, which was the case, and in the Soviet Union by mistake. They were allowed to return to Yugoslavia. In the early fifties they managed to obtain permission to leave the country ...

*

My father was able to escape from the prisoner of war camp in Klagenfurt in Austria without too much difficulty as I recall and to join us in the village of Grafenaschau, near the town of Murnau, in Bavaria....

*

In Murnau, we were moved into a school there and, after a short period of time, a refugee camp in a little village, Grafenaschau, five or six kilometres away. This camp was largely comprised of barracks which were shared by large numbers of individuals and families, who tried to create some kind of privacy by using such things as blankets to screen themselves off from the other occupants. While in this camp, I started attending a Russian school which was set up in the camp by some of the refugees. I managed to get excellent marks there and my command of Russian appears to have been very good, despite the fact that it is only my second language which I had started to learn only some six months before....

Not very long after we started living in the refugee camp, there occurred something which still fills me with emotion as I recall it. My father appeared suddenly near one of the barracks where I was playing with some children, dressed in an army overcoat, and we rushed towards each other and warmly hugged and kissed each other. I can still see in my mind's eye this event and the spot where it took place. My joy and that of my mother was immense, as we had not seen my father for something like nine months or more, and for nearly this whole period we did not know whether he was dead or alive. To see him alive and well was one of the happiest days of my life. My father gave me some sweets which he had been collecting for me while he was separated from us.

Our life in the camp came to an abrupt end some months later as we were expelled, along with the Sokolow family, because some of the refugees informed the camp authorities that my father and Sokolow had been members of the Russian Corps which fought alongside the German army. The Sokolows managed to find accommodation in a house which was not very far from the camp...

*

We left Germany for Australia late in 1949...

To pay off our mortgage as quickly as possible, my father took a second job and after the mortgage had been paid off he started campaigning for purchasing our own church. In the early 1950s, together with another member of the parish, he started collecting money from the community and within a short period of time they had collected a sufficient amount to put a deposit on a disused Anglican church in Collingwood, not far from the centre of the city. The church was in a pretty dilapidated state and my father and other members of the community had to do a lot of work to renovate it and make it fit for use. He put a lot of effort into the renovations himself. Subsequently, he became the Elder of the church and continued to spend a great deal of time and effort serving the church and the Russian community.

*

My father continued to live in the old people's home until he passed away in July 1989, on the feast day which is devoted to the Apostles Peter and Paul. Both of my parents were buried in the Russian part of Rockwood Cemetery in Sydney. A Russian Orthodox chapel is near their resting place and ceremonies for the deceased are held there on the appropriate days and attended by very large crowds of people....

Before my father passed away, he was hospitalized in the hospital in Lidcomb with sclerosis of the heart arteries. He was 86 at the time. From the hospital window one could see the cemetery where he would be buried. During his hospitalization in the Royal Canberra Hospital, in 1988, in a semi-delirious state he spoke about seeing a tombstone from his window, although there was no cemetery near that hospital, with his name on it and the year '1903 to...' He was never able to say what the latter year was.

During his hospitalization in Sydney my father spoke to me when I visited him, only a matter of days before he died, about seeing Czar Nicholas II and his family on the picture opposite his bed, although the picture was of a Spanish scene. Perhaps significantly, he was buried on the day which is devoted to a commemoration of their martyrdom. It is almost as if he saw something which would occur to him in the afterlife - being greeted in the next world by the Czar and his family as someone who had been a loyal and devoted servant of Russia and a virtuous and upright individual.

*

My father's influence on my life has been considerable. Whereas my mother provided overt love and emotional and moral support in great abundance, my father, through the way he brought me up, and personal example, instilled a strong sense of duty, perseverance, discipline and dedication. He was quite a stern man, and even slightly morose at times, but he was also loving and kind. My mother on the other hand, was not only very kind, but also very gentle.

*

Royal family c.1914. (Back) Maria, Olga, Tatiana, (middle)
Alexandra, Nicholas II, (children) Anastasia and Alexei.

Slava, born 12 February 1912, passed away on
31 January 1989.

Efimij, born on 30 January 1903, passed away shortly
after on 18 July 1989.

Alexander, born 23 November 1939, passed away
10 November 2009.

Their memory is treasured by their family in Canberra,
Australia.

C: Guide to Life-Guard regiments[24]

As at 1914.

- HER SOVEREIGN MAJESTY EMPRESS MARIA FEODOROVNA'S Chevalier Guards Regiment.
- Life-Guards Horse Regiment.
- HIS MAJESTY'S Life-Guards Cuirassier Regiment.
- HER SOVEREIGN MAJESTY EMPRESS MARIA FEODOROVNA'S Life-Guards Cuirassier Regiment.
- Life-Guards Horse-Grenadier Regiment.
- HER SOVEREIGN MAJESTY EMPRESS MARIA FEODOROVNA'S Life-Guards Lancer Regiment.
- Life-Guards Dragoon Regiment.
- HIS MAJESTY'S Life-Guards Hussar Regiment.
- HIS MAJESTY'S Life-Guards Lancer Regiment.
- Life-Guards Grodno Hussar Regiment.
- Life-Guards Horse Artillery.
  - 1st HIS MAJESTY'S Battery.
  - 2nd HIS IMPERIAL HIGHNESS General-Feldzeugmeister GRAND DUKE MICHAEL NIKOLAEVICH'S Battery.

---

[24] Mark Conrad, 2001, *Standing divisions of the Russian Army 1914*, http://marksrussianmilitaryhistory.info/RUSS1914.html#CAVAL RY

- o 3rd HIS IMPERIAL HIGHNESS GRAND DUKE GEORGE MIKHAILOVICH'S Battery.
- o 4th HIS IMPERIAL HIGHNESS THE HEIR AND TSESAREVICH GRAND DUKE ALEXEI NIKOLAEVICH'S battery.
- o 5th HIS IMPERIAL HIGHNESS GRAND DUKE MICHAEL ALEKSANDROVICH'S Battery.
- o 6th HIS MAJESTY'S L.-Gds. Don Cossack Battery.

Cossack and other irregular troops:

- HIS MAJESTY'S Life-Guards Cossack Regiment.
- HIS IMPERIAL HIGHNESS THE SOVEREIGN HEIR AND TSESAREVICH'S Life-Guards Ataman Regiment.
- Life-Guards Combined Cossack Regiment.
  - o 1st HIS MAJESTY'S Ural Sotnia.
  - o 2nd Orenburg Sotnia.
  - o 3rd Combined Sotnia.
  - o 4th Amur Sotnia.
- 6th HIS MAJESTY'S L.-Gds. Don Cossack Battery.

D: Rough guide to Russian ranks

Trooper	рядовой
Lance-Corporal	ефрейтор
Corporal (NCO)	младший унтер-офицер
Sergeant (NCO)	старший унтер-офицер
Wachtmeister (NCO)	вахмистр
Cornet	корнет
Lieutenant	поручик
Staff Captain	штабс-ротмистр
Captain	ротмистр
Major	майо́р
Lieutenant Colonel	подполковник
Colonel	полковник
Major General	генерал-майор
Lieutenant General	генерал-лейтенант
General	генерал от кавалерии

Index

Made in the USA
Lexington, KY
28 July 2015